Contents

Disclaimer

Names of some of the people and places mentioned have been changed to protect the privacy of individuals.

The author wishes to stress that the views portrayed are based on recollections of some thirty years ago and that she writes from the position of an outside observer.

– 1 –
Setting Out

In the early 1960s most Australian whites knew and cared little about the situation of the Aborigines. Even the well-meaning tended to be fairly ignorant, many supporting the policy of assimilation on the grounds that the embarrassing evidence of what we had done to the original inhabitants would disappear once their race was absorbed into ours. Others were vituperative on the subject, blaming the problems on the Aborigines themselves, classing them as being by nature unintelligent, lazy and undeserving.

My family belonged to the group who read with horror the stories of early massacres and cruelties and felt sympathy for those we saw living on the fringes of our towns, without being able to see a solution to their problems. Their land was gone, their former natural way of life could never be restored; the status quo had been established and nothing more could be done to alter it. I grew up quite unaware that there was a Government policy on Aborigines. What an eye-opener it was then to spend two years living on a Government Reserve and to see first hand how this 'Welfare Board' so often belied its name.

My childhood had been largely spent in a small coastal town. Several black families lived on the outskirts but they did not impinge much on our lives. One old lady who worked for my mother as a washerwoman had grown up on a riverside reserve known as Yellow Rock. As white settlers took over the valley, a large Aboriginal community had been herded into this one small area by the Aboriginal Protection Board. There they were ruled over by a manager. As kids we used to row across to Yellow Rock and wander among the rusty relics of the abandoned mission imagining that this way of life belonged to our early history.

We saw the young Aborigines from the town growing up in much the same way as we were, enjoying the same carefree existence where swimming, fishing and sport absorbed all our time and attention. We never stopped to wonder why they didn't go to the Saturday night dances as they got older, why they attended sports days and played in the town football team but never came along to the parties afterwards. That was so much a fact of life that to question it was inconceivable. It was taken for granted too that none of them would go to high school, and that when they left, the menial jobs of the district would be their lot.

When I returned as a teacher in the 'fifties nothing much had changed. A few little black faces stood out among the whites in the classroom and mingled as happily with them in the playground as their elders did on the football field. The post-war years were prosperous, life had resumed its usual sleepy routine; all was well.

One of our local heroes was Andy Boney who had risen to the rank of sergeant during the war and was much fêted on Anzac Day. Indeed he was welcome in the bar any day; he was a great bloke, for a black. He had a good job, he was clean and respectable, and had even been written up in the papers. People felt good talking to him. It showed what big-hearted folk we all were, didn't it? No one could accuse our town of prejudice. It was Andy who first gave me an inkling that things were not accepted as passively as we had thought.

I was struggling from the railway station one evening with a large suitcase when Andy caught up. He insisted on carrying my case all the way home and as we were talking he mentioned a family with whom I was friendly. He said that they were the only really unprejudiced family in town. I protested that everyone liked him . . . he was one of our respected citizens.

'Oh yes,' he answered, 'I'm good old Andy. I get asked in for a drink sometimes. But no one but Mrs Griffiths has ever asked my wife and kids to visit.' His voice grew bitter and mocking. 'People don't mind us blacks, you know. They just want us to keep in our place.'

I felt guilty about it and looked at the little black faces in the class with new knowledge. They played quite happily now with the others, but it would not be too many years before they would have to learn to keep to their allotted place, the bottom rung of the social and economic ladder.

After a few years I married another teacher, Neil Keating, and we moved to a small school in a pretty valley among the coastal hills where I proceeded to have five children in record time. The twins, Anne and Beth, were followed in a little over a year by Peter. Then came Christopher and barely twelve months later, Megan. Naturally I was completely absorbed and overwhelmed by family matters in those fecund years. All other concerns and causes faded into the background and I was submerged in a world of nappies and bottles and demanding baby voices. I vaguely knew that there was a big Aboriginal community in Taree about an hour's drive away, but I rarely saw or heard of them. And when I did they seemed quite happy, so I took it for granted that all was well in the land of the 'fair go'.

Then in 1962 Neil received an offer of promotion to a two-teacher school near Yarrawina, on the western plains. The school was on a Government Aboriginal Reserve and had a residence available. It was the first time we really had become aware of these reserves and were intrigued by the novelty of the situation.

We had been quite happy in the small farming community but the lure of change and adventure beckoned, and besides it was a promotion and thus more money. It was a struggle on the pittance paid to a junior teacher, so we gathered our courage and accepted. Borrowing a hundred pounds from my sister and her husband, we set off with about as much foresight and knowledge as our gold-seeking great-grandfathers when they went west a hundred years before. Dire warnings and prophecies of doom accompanied us. My father-in-law bitterly forecast not only the ruination of his son's career but the blighting of the lives of his five grandchildren.

So with our small Vauxhall packed and the trailer loaded with bedding, food and a tent we headed across the ranges and western slopes, camping for a night in the bush, cooking on an open fire, singing songs, telling stories and playing 'I spy'. The children loved it and slept soundly on their camp beds. Then with the first rays of sun we were up to prepare food for the day, sterilise the baby's bottles, wash the nappies and follow the sun across the plains.

It became hotter and drier; the children began the plaint 'How much longer?' and fiercely disputed their territories in the back seat, while eight-month-old Megan fretted and squirmed on my knee. The novelty of the trip had worn off and we were now intent on one thing only — getting there. Visions of cool showers and comfortable beds beckoned us on.

Neil and the children

– 2 –
Arrival

It was a hot, still February day and our apprehension increased with every mile we travelled. The countryside grew browner, flatter, drier. Trees were sparse and stunted and the few houses we passed seemed isolated and insignificant, dwarfed by the monotonous sameness of the plains that stretched away endlessly under a huge sky. The children were uncomfortable and fretful and Neil and I sat in gloomy silence, neither of us willing to voice our suspicion that we had made a fearful mistake.

We arrived at Yarrawina about noon and our first glimpse of the town brought extravagant relief. We drove past the outlying houses and sheds and down the wide main street lined with old-style wooden buildings, their ornate architecture recalling the town's former glory as an important river port, and their drab, unpainted surfaces proclaiming its present decline into insignificance.

While Neil shopped and asked directions to the Mission I bought ice-creams and supervised their consumption. The children were silent and absorbed, savouring this rare luxury and I had time to look around. The town was not as deserted as it first appeared. People strolled along the shaded footpaths and leaned against the posts supporting the wide verandah awnings. Groups lounged under the trees in the small park and a few teenagers gathered outside the milk bar, fingers clicking, feet moving in unison to the music blaring through the door. Then I realised with a surge of excitement that most of them were black. This town was certainly different from all others we had known and that had been one of our reasons for coming. We forgot the heat and dust and, setting off across the bridge on the last ten miles of the journey, we recaptured some of the zest with which we had started.

We headed back on the gravel road for a few miles and then turned off onto a black soil track that wound through miles of grey-green scrub. The children were wide awake and excited and we all chattered happily about the joys of reaching our new house. The prospect of leaving the cramped car and spending an afternoon relaxing was enough to raise everyone's spirits. Then we saw it, a few buildings clustered among the trees. We had arrived. A notice on a high wire fence informed us we were entering Government property and should seek permission before proceeding further. We crawled across the grid and drove in.

On our left stood a group of buildings painted in Government cream and brown, shaded by a few pepper trees. One was obviously a hall and it was flanked by a shed and a small building labelled 'clinic'. The school stood behind them, separated from the others by a large bare playground. On the right, scarcely visible through the trees and shrubs that adorned its lawns, we saw a house with wide verandahs and imposing chimneys. A notice on the white picket fence pointed to a side entrance that led to the office. We drew up under a tree and sat staring in amazed silence at the bizarre scene ahead.

A large clearing stretched out to the distant walls of bush. It was brown and bare, studded with a few straggling trees and groups of small, shed-like buildings made from corrugated iron and fibro. The sun was reflected back from these in shimmering waves and it took a few seconds to realise that they were houses, set in tiny yards with broken fences. They lined a grid of dirt streets with gaps here and there where the rubble of former buildings still lay. It was still and silent, and the sun seemed to have drained all colour away, leaving a landscape as stark and harsh as a Drysdale painting. Then in the patches of shade beside the houses and under the trees we could see figures moving and hear the murmur of voices. The realisation that there were people present, and that they were most likely scrutinising us with matching curiousity, jolted us out of our mesmerised state. Neil set off to find the office while I, looking from the stately home beside us to the ramshackle sheds in front, tried to work out which of the buildings would be our new home.

Then Neil reappeared looking perplexed. He announced that we had not been expected as the previous teachers had lived in Yarrawina. After years of emptiness and neglect the 'teacher's house' had fallen into disrepair and would need cleaning and restoring if we insisted on staying. The Manager had not been very optimistic about our chances of moving straight into a house in town either, he added. It might mean staying in one of the hotels for a while.

'We can't do that,' I wailed. 'I can't mind all the kids in a hotel. We can't afford it anyhow. And what about our furniture? It's due today. Where will we put it?'

My lament was interrupted by the appearance of the Manager. Neil introduced him and my spirits lifted. He was a handsome young man, smartly dressed, softly spoken, beautifully mannered, and he was an Aborigine — surely evidence that a new order had arrived. This must be a great new experiment in equality, I thought. Here we would see the Aboriginal people managing their own affairs, unfettered by white domination, and I wanted to be there to bear witness.

I quickly advanced all my reasons for wanting to stay at the Mission and faced with such determination, however illogical, Neil agreed. The Manager seemed less than impressed by our decision. When his arguments for our departure proved unavailing he coldly requested that the children and I remain in the car while he showed Neil the house. They went off towards a building half-hidden by a few sparse trees. I could see its rusty red roof and unpainted walls and noted with delight that it was slightly isolated, standing alone near a line of bigger trees that marked the course of the river.

After an anxious wait I saw Neil striding back towards us, his face grim. He described the sagging walls, the broken flywire, the peeling paint. He mentioned the missing floorboards on the verandah, the old black fuel stove in the kitchen and the wash tubs in the back yard laundry.

'*And* there's no electricity', he muttered darkly. 'A generator supplies enough power for lights, but that's all. There is no electric stove, no fridge, no iron, no washing machine. Now what do you want to do? Move into town and beg for accommodation, or resign or what?'

I couldn't answer for a moment. Then I saw the twins gazing anxiously at us, stricken more by the harshness of Neil's voice than his actual words. So I managed to conjure up a feeble smile and murmur, 'No, the electricity doesn't matter. We'll manage. I'd rather stay'. He strode off morosely.

All that long, hot afternoon I debated my sanity. Figures hurried to and fro from the house; the sounds of hammering and banging were evidence of repairs under way. I longed to go over and become involved but feared a rebuff. Then the furniture truck arrived, unloaded and departed. The driver stopped by the car on the way out. He gloomily forecast that we'd move out in a few weeks.

'Nobody could live in a place like that,' he added. 'It's only fit for the blacks. What do you think you're doing, bringing those little kids out to this dump?'

My morale plummeted even further. I fed the children on fruit and biscuits and told them their favourite stories till they dozed off. I was craving a cup of tea. Surely someone would offer me one. All the legends of country hospitality began with an invitation to a 'cuppa'. But no one appeared and I was contemplating boiling up the billy on our little primus stove when Megan woke up and insisted on her bottle. It was already prepared in the icebox and only needed warming so I unearthed it and searched through the trailer for the primus. It was, of course, firmly wedged under a mound of camping gear. I decided to put these stories of lavish hospitality to the test. After assuring Megan and her two patient big sisters that I'd be back in a moment I made my way through the garden clutching the ice-cold bottle. I really expected that I would be asked to bring the children in out of the heat, even if only as far as the verandah or the garden. And of course I'd be offered a drink of some description.

I knocked on the front door and it opened promptly. A woman in her late twenties stood there, dressed in a neat print frock and sensible lace-up shoes. Her light brown hair was scraped back behind her ears in an uncompromising straight bob that added to the severity of her expression. I introduced myself and chattered on about the house and the long wait and the necessity of heating the bottle. I faltered to a stop as her pale blue eyes took in my tousled hair, the crumpled skirt and blouse and my old sandals. Then she smiled briefly and introduced herself in turn as Shirley, the Manager's wife. She took the bottle and disappeared inside. I waited on the verandah and through the half-open door I could see the gleaming floor of the wide hallway and a corner of the formal dining room. The smell of beeswax polish and the dark interior reminded me of convent parlours in my youth and I felt the same sense of being an intruder on hallowed ground.

Then Shirley was back with the suitably warmed bottle. She told me she would arrange for a kerosene refrigerator and a petrol iron to be sent to the house. We could use them till we got our own. She acknowledged my effusive thanks with another frosty smile and closed the door. I returned to the car where a crowd of small dark children now clustered, joining with my five in the hilarious giggling, shrieking and showing off that constitute the introductory rites of childhood. They scattered as I approached, but soon drifted back accompanied by a few teenagers. This older group responded reluctantly at first to my conversational overtures but the antics of the younger children, as they strutted and capered to amuse us, soon broke down their formal reserve. Though they sat with their faces averted and their eyes downcast most of the time, they answered my questions politely, flashing me shy smiles as they spoke. Each answer was the signal for a gust of chatter and laughter among themselves. Their sideways glances let me know that this was for my benefit and that they were gauging my reactions to what they said so I was carefully non-committal and learnt quite a lot. I found that the 'Boss' and 'Matron' loomed large in their lives.

They were, of course, the Manager and his wife and they were regarded as supreme authority figures, not only dispensing the necessities of life, but acting as the guardians of civil and moral law as well.

My questions about the school brought an embarrassed silence until one girl voiced the opinion that it was boring and she couldn't wait to leave. The chorus of comments that followed all pointed to its irrelevance to their life now, and to any future work prospects. They seemed surprised that I should see any connection between school and jobs. Another pretty young lass said she had left school before Christmas and was working in the laundry on the Mission till her mother let her leave to get work in town or on a station. I was pleased to hear that there was work available on the Mission and envisaged the 'laundry' as a commercial proposition run by the Aborigines themselves, most likely servicing the local hospital and hotels. It was good, I thought, that there was a source of income and employment, and I was about to enquire further when I noticed Neil and the Manager approaching. My little group instantly and silently dispersed. However, I heard with relief that the house was ready and we could move in.

We drove over and parked at the front gate. The setting sun cast a pink glow on the shabby walls and roof and as we unloaded the children the house seemed a welcoming haven. We went in carrying the two sleepy babies with the three eldest, silent and wide-eyed, following behind. The Manager had lined up his group of cleaners and repair men in the kitchen to meet us. There were eight of them, standing in a semi-circle. Their dark expressionless faces and unwavering scrutiny gave an impression of resentment, even of hostility. We were introduced and Neil gave a short speech thanking them for their help. Then each of them had to step forward to be introduced individually. It was like a reception line and as we shook hands and murmured greetings they all responded with brief smiles before stepping back into line. Their faces then resumed expressions of stolid indifference. After all they had just spent hours making things comfortable for a white family they had neither invited nor welcomed.

We assumed that they would be paid for the afternoon's work and it was sometime before we found out that, except for the handyman and the clinic assistant, no one on the Mission was paid for any labour around the place. The others in the group were indigents, those with no income at all, who paid for their share of the Government's bounty by obedience to any command of the Boss. And if that command resulted in long, hot hours of toil on our behalf they were expected to comply without demur.

Then they all departed and we were left alone in our strange old house. The basic furniture was in place but the sheets, blankets, crockery and household utensils were still packed in the boxes lining the verandah. Rather than face unpacking, Neil set up the camp stove in the kitchen for our first meal while I made up the beds with our camping blankets. Soon the exhausted children were fed and bedded down in rooms that were still damp and reeked of disinfectant.

We were alone and I was able to indulge in the flood of hysterical tears that had threatened for hours. Fortunately Neil was able to produce a small flask of whiskey from one of the boxes. Its sharp pungency had the desired effect and sanity returned. By now it was dark and we went out to sit on the verandah looking over the straggling village. Light shone out from the Big House and what seemed to be candles flickered fitfully in the windows of some of the huts. A few indistinct figures moved occasionally between the buildings, and voices and laughter sounded randomly. Dogs barked and someone whistled a monotonous tune. As the darkness thickened the silence grew and the main sound was the muted chugging of the generator charging the batteries for the lights. Then it stopped. The moon rose and the little houses looked like cardboard cut-outs in its clear light. Nothing stirred and as we sat staring into the night the haunting plaint of a curlew and the whine of mosquitoes provided a fitting background to our dismal thoughts. We felt as though we had landed on an alien shore where the hardships were much greater than expected and the welcome much less.

Yet the next morning brought a resurgence of good spirits.

The back verandah overlooked a bend of the river. Its brown water gleamed between high clay banks and, as we watched, a kangaroo hopped slowly from the edge to disappear into the bush opposite the house. A blue crane flapped lazily upstream and landed on a branch overhanging the water and a family of ducks slid past.

Except for the outdoor toilet, a shed-like structure, and one bedraggled tree, the yard was bare. The soil was cracked and dry, supporting only a few clumps of blue-grey weeds, but we optimistically decided it could be transformed into a garden without too much trouble. The house itself wasn't too bad either we agreed. It was basically a four-roomed square, split by a wide hallway that ran from front to back.

The rooms were big and airy and there was a broad verandah all around. One part of it had been closed in and would make a room just big enough for the two boys. The walls had faded to grey and the floors were covered with green Government-issue lino in reasonable repair. It had a cool, pleasant atmosphere and, in our new buoyant mood, that was more important than that the walls sloped erratically and shook as we moved around. The missing floorboards on the verandahs and the tattered fly-screens were offset by the neat brick fireplace that stood in the lounge room and even the black fuel stove dominating the kitchen looked inviting when Neil lit the fire.

We unpacked some of the boxes and began to cook our first proper meal while the children delved into the open crates, ecstatically greeting their possessions like long-lost and almost forgotten friends. The general euphoria lasted while we fed and dressed the children, washing them in the baby's bath on the sunny verandah. The eldest three raced excitedly out into the yard and leapt back almost immediately, howling with pain. Their bare feet were studded with 'cat-heads': hard, needle-sharp burrs. Here was no lush green grass on which to run barefoot, so thongs and sandals had to be worn outside. We soon learned to leave outdoor footwear on the steps, together with the snake sticks that were propped at each door.

The first morning whirled by as we unpacked and stowed the goods we needed. Neil had to make a quick trip to town for more supplies and came back with the car loaded with groceries and a head full of facts he had garnered in the two hours he was away. Facts about the weather, the shopping arrangements, the social life of the town and, of course, the Aborigines. He reeled off the local white lore: we would be robbed and conned by the 'abos'; they were dirty, smelly and spread disease; he would not be able to teach them anything because of their low intelligence; and they only respected forceful authority, meaning that he should use the cane vigorously. He had discovered most of this information over a drink in the hotel and I was not surprised by this familiar diatribe. However, I was perturbed by the news from the shopkeeper that there was no fresh milk available at any time and that fruit and vegetables came in only on Thursday, not exactly in pristine condition after a long truck ride from the market gardens of South Australia. I imagined that the children, reared on rich Jersey milk and home-grown vegetables of the coast, would fade away. They didn't of course but it took me a long time to overcome my suspicions of powdered milk.

Then Neil began to unload the car. He staggered in with drums of kerosene, a fifty-pound bag of flour, a great sack of sugar and several huge tins of powdered milk. The friendly shop-owner had advised him to buy in bulk as even a small storm would make the road impassable, and if the rains set in, we could be isolated for weeks. We had to keep the pantry well stocked, Neil advised me, so that I could whip up dampers as a bread substitute and churn out biscuits and scones and other home-made delicacies. I doubted that my paltry culinary skills would ever cope with a damper and, as I tried to sieve the lumps from a jug of milk I had just made up, I felt great sympathy for the pioneer women, not because of the perils they faced, but for having to cook for their families so far from any shops.

The Manager and his wife visited us after lunch. They brought along their two attractive school-aged children who entertained ours while their parents got acquainted. We offered tea or coffee but they declined because of their religious beliefs and we sat chatting stiffly around the kitchen table. I was conscious of Shirley eyeing the cane chairs that were the only real articles of furniture we had in the lounge room and I knew she was not fooled by the bright cloth covering the tea chest that masqueraded as a coffee table. This evidence of our unprepossessing lifestyle must have been reinforced when I produced a packet of tobacco and deftly rolled a smoke. Her face grew stern and her answers became monosyllabic. As she sat, straight-backed and still with her hands in her lap, I was reminded once again of the convent school and Reverend Mother's austere appearance as she judged and found me wanting. We were to find Shirley's apparent hauteur was really a mask to conceal her insecurity and vulnerability, but it certainly dampened down any conversational overtures during the first part of the afternoon.

Len, however, seemed quite at ease as he instructed us in the mores of the Mission. We learnt that all visitors must report to him and he had the power to admit or refuse them entry; we should not fraternise too freely with the inhabitants; all correspondence relating to the place must be sent through him and no liquor was to be brought onto the reserve. When Neil cavilled at this, protesting that he liked a beer in the evening, Len laughed and agreed that the prohibition didn't really apply to teachers or even Managers or other welfare officers. But he warned us against offering a drink to an Aborigine as most of them were not allowed liquor under the Aboriginal Protection Act and it was strictly taboo on any reserve. We agreed to all these strictures, even though, it seemed that perhaps some had been formulated more to restrain than to protect the residents.

The conversation became more general and Len told us about his job and the problems he faced. He was among the first Aborigines to be employed by the Welfare Board in any sort of executive position and he faced an onerous task. For one thing he was resented by the local black people. Not only was he a stranger from the coast, but he was regarded as a turncoat, an Aborigine who had sided with white authority. He was quite philosophical about their attitude, acknowledging that as it arose from years of repression, it would take years to change. His second concern was more immediate but also more easily solved. It was his lack of formal education. He had been to school on the reserve where he grew up and, as was usual, had been taught by the Manager, who had neither the time nor the training to teach more than the absolute basics. Consequently Len was largely self-educated and in spite of his obvious intelligence was having trouble with the many written reports required in his job. When Neil offered the advice that the best way to develop a fluent writing style was to read widely and constantly, Len became interested and asked for help in starting a suitable program. They began to sort through our books with enthusiasm.

With the men engrossed in their pursuit of good literature, Shirley and I were left to explore more domestic topics. We soon embarked on what was apparently her favourite subject, the iniquities of the local Aborigines. I was surprised at her violent condemnation as I had expected a great measure of tolerance from one who had flouted white society's ultimate taboo — marriage with a black person. However, it emerged that most of the local Aborigines were not only slothful and disrespectful, but they were utterly depraved morally. I was horrified until I realised that they were being judged from the narrow viewpoint of a strict religious sect. Their fondness for gambling, a trait shared by most Australians, could hardly be classed as depravity, especially as the gambling consisted of playing cards for matches or bottletops. Shirley however, considered it sufficiently criminal to warrant late-night raids on suspect houses and to merit the use of eviction threats as a deterrent.

Shirley was quick to assure me that there were 'good' Aborigines, even among the river-bank dwellers, but they were outnumbered by the 'cheeky' ones. We were to become familiar with these terms as part of the Welfare Board jargon. They apparently denoted the division of the Aborigines into those who were obedient and subservient and those who were prone to question the Board's authority. It soon became clear that Neil was expected to train the next generation to join the former group.

The afternoon ended with mutual goodwill. Len urged us to use his office phone, the only one on the reserve, to ring our orders through to the shops. He would then bring out our groceries on his regular trips to town to get the Mission supplies.

He pointed out the canvas-roofed truck that was the sole means of transport to and from town. He suggested that we should not upset the status quo by offering the people lifts in our car. The 'gubbie truck', as it was called, was available for their use and it was a way of keeping track of their movements.

Then Shirley offered us a supply of basic groceries and cleaning materials. They were supplied in bulk, she said, and we were welcome to replenish our stock from the storeroom. Realising that these were meant for the Aborigines, we were taken aback and managed to stammer a grateful refusal. Then she plunged us into deeper embarrassment by offering to send us a girl to help with the housework. Again we demurred politely, saying we would see about it when we were settled. With the parlous state of our finances the last thing we could afford was the luxury of a maid, I thought privately.

They left amicably with an invitation on our part to 'drop in any time' and a gracious admission from Shirley that it was nice to have someone to talk to at last. Len carried off his armful of books, his face alight with enthusiasm, promising to start on them that night. We watched them walk away, their children — slim and dark, like their father — dancing between them.

Peter, holding the football, with the local team

– 3 –

Getting Acquainted

That evening Neil worked in the school and the children and I went for a walk around the village. The houses were even more wretched close up. They were no more than shacks built of corrugated iron and sheets of broken fibro, verandahless oblongs with fireplaces tacked on one end. They crouched low on the bare ground surrounded by remnants of wire fences that enclosed a woodheap, a lavatory and occasionally a few straggling plants. There were two doors and a couple of windows that opened by propping out sheets of iron with sticks. Refinements such as glass or flyscreens were non-existent and the only adornment was the white paint that had been applied, obviously many years before, to the front walls. The other walls and the roof remained in their original state, their surfaces embellished only by rust and the dark stains of age and neglect. We were later told that this paint had been applied before the visit of some dignitary, perhaps a State Governor, who drove along the street waving graciously to the inhabitants lined up before their sparkling white houses.

I hope he noticed the water taps sticking up at intervals along the street and realised their significance. These were the only source of water for the Aborigines. It was piped directly from the river and had to be carried in buckets from the communal taps. This was no incentive to cleanliness and must have added to the drudgery of wash day, as well as precluding any serious attempt at gardening.

A few of the houses had been improved a little, with simple timber awnings to provide shade and small tanks or drums to catch rain water. Here the fences were in good repair and there were small garden plots. But even these minor additions cost money and so indicated that these houses were occupied by families with men working on nearby stations as shearers or casual labourers. Their homes reflected their small measure of economic independence. The others, the indigents, were totally dependent on the Government and their houses reflected their landlord's callous lack of interest. When eventually I did get invited into one of the houses, I was appalled by the dirt floors, the lack of basic furniture and the absence of any of the amenities that we take for granted. But that invitation came much later when we had established a firm base of trust and friendship. These people had enough pride to wish to hide their pitiful living conditions from casual acquaintances.

On this first outing the children and I were watched with much curiosity and not a little amusement. After all there had been no white people living at such close quarters before and it was not often that white people looked as impotent and frustrated as I did while trying to manoeuvre the overladen pram among the potholes. Christopher had refused to join the three eldest children who pranced along beside me. He was convinced the burrs would attack him, even through his sturdy shoes, and I had perched him in the pram with Megan. The additional weight threatened to bring the whole expedition to a halt when we reached a deeply rutted intersection. Then one of the girls I had met the day before came out of the nearest house, and greeting me shyly, helped us out of the pot-holes. Some of her family followed and a few neighbours drifted across. An initial, awkward silence was soon dispelled as Anne and Beth, delighted to find a new audience, began to regale them with tales of our family doings. Peter ran off with the small boys who soon became his inseparable companions. Megan and Christopher were lifted from the pram and much admired while I chatted to the circle of adults. I was so relieved to be met with welcoming smiles and genuine interest and to be able to revise my gloomy forebodings of the night before.

As we walked home through the dusk I was well-pleased with life. What did the lack of amenities matter? There were more things in life than labour-saving devices. That thought was qualified a short time later however, as I tried to light the old chip heater over the bath. It was a cylindrical tank with a space for paper and kindling. When this was lit the draught up the chimney soon had the fire blazing and the water heating. It was quite efficient but puffed and snorted like a steam train. With the children watching open-mouthed, I tried to disguise my fears of an explosion, but the increasing *whoof whoof whoof* roar soon nullified my shaky assurances and they broke and ran. It took some minutes to gather them up and many more to persuade them that it was safe to get in the bath, especially as the water gushing in was a dark, peaty brown. It was the first time they had tried the river water. It was almost opaque and had a rich, earthy smell. Traces of mud remained in the bottom of the bath when the plug was pulled and I wondered what it would taste like. Thank goodness we had a tank. Then I remembered those taps in the street.

The real test of my new philosophy came the next morning when I faced my first full-scale washday. As usual we rose early. Neil was anxious to get to school and prepare for the traumatic first day. He lit the fires in the kitchen and the laundry, gulped down a quick breakfast and was gone. I fed and dressed everyone, and leaving them ensconced on the verandah with books and toys, ventured to attack the mountain of washing soaking in the rough cement tubs. These stood beside the great fire-belching copper under a lean-to roof in the back yard. Then began the ordeal of the good old-fashioned washday: the soaping and scrubbing in the first tub, rinsing in the second, flinging the clothes into the boiling copper to be prodded, stirred and heaved into a basket to await the mandatory two rinses. I knew how to do it all right. Childhood memories came flooding back: the smell of steaming wet clothes, the hiss of water dripping onto the sides of the copper, the cool blue of the last rinse. But I couldn't remember Mum getting as wet and soot-streaked as I was now.

By the time the last load was pegged on the line I was reeling from exhaustion and hoarse from shouting orders at the children. Freed from close supervision, and aware that I seemed inextricably stuck on the washing-cycle treadmill, they had invaded the woodheap, the car shed, the tank-stand and other perilous places. I rounded them up and we tip-toed past the sleeping baby tucked up on a rug on the verandah. I had just stoked up the kitchen fire and put the kettle on when I saw Shirley striding down our path.

Immaculate in her white uniform, she surveyed the chaos, the dirty children and their dirtier mother, and the unwashed dishes in the sink. Her disapproval was obvious but that did not deter her from sitting stolidly for two hours while I desperately tried to restore order, prepare lunch and converse at the same time. And so began a routine that annoyed me intensely for the first few months. After attending to her duties in the clinic and the storeroom Shirley would fill in the remaining hours of the morning by visiting me. She told me tales of the incompetence of her workers, the transgressions committed by so many of her charges and the clever sayings of her superiors in the Welfare Board.

Gradually I learnt to cope with Shirley's visits. By continuing with the housework around her immobile figure, I managed to clean, cook and attend to the children while she talked on, her voice merely background noise like a radio. As her religion forbade tea and coffee, and I did not keep soft drinks or cordial in the house, I was spared the ritual of the 'cuppa' and I soon learnt to start early on the heavy chores, leaving myself time for a fortifying coffee before she arrived. Neil was most unsympathetic, accusing me of moral cowardice because I could not summon up sufficient ruthlessness to terminate the visits. However, I did find one way of shortening them. Shirley had many real aversions, ranging from minor concerns like dancing, make-up and smoking to more fundamental matters of race and religion. I could usually stop a harangue by defending one of these, causing her to leave in disgust. But in true missionary spirit she would always return next day, except for the occasion when she discovered I was both a Catholic and a champion of women's rights. However, even these horrifying revelations earned me only a few days' blissful respite.

From her visits though I learned a lot about the workings of the Welfare Board. Many of those who worked with Aborigines seemed to heartily dislike them, but an unsettling discovery was the numbers of untrained personnel. One of the most senior men was reputed to have completed only one year of an anthropology course, but many others seemed to have been garnered from all walks of life regardless of aptitude or previous qualifications. Managers in charge of hundreds of people on the reserves had the power to drastically affect the lives of their charges, splitting families, banishing 'undesirables' and acting in fact as prosecutor, judge and jury, with little chance of appeal against their decisions. They had undertaken no training courses in psychology or social work to assist them in this procedure. We knew of one who had taken up the job because a bad back prevented him from staying on in his real work as a carpenter. Len himself would have benefited greatly, both in confidence and competence, had he been fully prepared. The rank above the Managers, the District Officers, rated no better and the whole department seemed to be largely staffed by amateurs. No doubt many of them were intelligent and compassionate and learnt through experience to do a competent job but some were there only because it was an occupation that required neither aptitude nor training.

We frequently met two District Officers. They had awesome powers over the Aborigines living in a large part of the State. One was a migrant with past connections to the British army in India. He mostly managed to disguise his disdain for all things Australian, particularly Aborigines, but one evening as he shared a few of our beers he argued that Neil was doing the wrong thing by trying to raise educational standards at the school. 'An educated black is a cheeky black,' he stated and expounded on the problems that were created by educating them above their 'station in life'. Perhaps he had been attracted to the job by earlier memories of a servant class or his experiences as a white conqueror in a colonial country.

The second officer was an even more unfortunate choice, a

burly, brusque woman who seemed to believe that insults were a form of wit and that you were a bad sport if you did not accept them amicably. Her most derogatory epithet was 'do-gooder' one she flung at me on a number of occasions. She did not attempt to disguise her scorn for the blacks and apparently thought that her mission in life was to keep her unfortunate charges from ever coming to the notice of the outside world. Any complaints about their treatment she regarded as treachery to the Welfare Board. It was evident that in her eyes the Aborigines existed only to support that body, not the other way around. The Superior Pom and Madam Gestapo, as we privately termed them, were frequent visitors for a time, more in quest of refreshment than for any love of our company. However, after my furious denunciation of her callousness about the deaths of several black babies in a nearby reserve, Madam left my morning tea table in high dudgeon. From that time we were spared any unofficial visits from Welfare Board personnel.

One of the most appalling examples of lack of training was Shirley herself. As she dispensed medicines and advice for ailments like the flu, gastric troubles and infectious childhood diseases, I took it for granted that she would have had some basic nursing training. And as she supervised the health and welfare of the babies and advised their mothers, I thought that the course would have dealt intensively with nutrition and mothercraft. However, she had no medical training whatsoever and her only work experience was some years as a domestic servant in a private house. Even with the knowledge gained from having two children of her own the position of Matron in charge of a clinic surely required more expertise than Shirley possessed. The responsibilities thrust upon her were unfair and frightening, although she did not think so, and she made her pronouncements with the confidence born of sheer ignorance.

Coping with Shirley became an obsession. I soon realised that her visits did not stem from any liking for my company. I apparently annoyed her more than she irritated me; but she had no one else. She could not bridge the gap separating her from her charges, and as I was the only other woman around, my kitchen became her substitute for the 'back fence' of the bored suburban housewife. Her children were at school, Len was usually busy and she wasn't interested in reading. But unlike most wives she could not fill her day with work. Those women I saw moving around the house and the men we glimpsed in the garden were a team of domestic servants a nineteenth-century squire would have envied. The girl who boasted about leaving school to work in the laundry was not in any commercial establishment. She was now one of a small group who laboured over the washing and ironing at the Big House. No wonder Shirley's family was always immaculate and spruce.

After a few weeks, life settled into a routine. Neil was wallowing under a mountain of work at the school which had suffered under the same policy of careless neglect that had affected the rest of the place. Standards were low and keeping order seemed to be the only priority. Academic standards applying to white schools had no relevance here. He was delighted however by his assistant, Merrita, an attractive, competent girl who had applied especially for a position teaching Aborigines. Her enthusiasm and vivacity made her an instant favourite with both the children and their parents and she became our closest friend and confidant. She lived in town and drove out in all weathers in her little yellow Volkswagen; the car became a familiar and welcome sight as it whizzed along towards the Mission, mud-spattered or covered in dust.

While Neil and Merrita worked enthusiastically on school problems, I was gradually learning the conventions of this new community. The people were friendly and polite but for the first few months I seemed to be looking at the complex social structure of the Mission from a distance and I felt isolated. It was like watching a theatrical performance by fascinating characters and not understanding the plot. The children however had speedily adapted to their new surroundings. This was the first time they had ever lived near other families and they were delighted to find a flock of pre-schoolers who ran and played in seemingly unfettered freedom. They joined the group happily and were readily accepted. At first I worried when they wandered out of sight and panicked badly the first time I saw them all disappearing down the path to the river. I ran after them, upset and angry, and was met by two smiling women who told me not to worry. They were keeping an eye on the youngsters, one added, and would see they kept out of harm.

Theirs was a truly communal life and the sharing was not only of material goods, but of time and responsibility. The women cared as readily for all the children as they did for their own and there was no pay-back or roster system. Mothers who were sick or busy or had been called away knew that their families would function quite satisfactorily in their absence and they in turn were always ready to contribute equally to the common good. My children were accepted freely into this protective system, so that on the two occasions I was not able to look after them because of illness, they did not miss a beat. They were cared for and comforted while Neil was at work and it was all done so unobtrusively that it was hard to know who to thank. It was this matter-of-fact practical help, completely lacking in any overtones of dutiful charity, that I missed most when we returned to so-called civilisation.

Because they believed themselves to be unsupervised by adults, the children felt wonderfully free and independent. They made their own decisions and settled their own squabbles. The physical environment presented plenty of challenges and there were enough imaginary dangers to stimulate and thrill the most adventurous. However, there were always adults nearby to give comfort, first aid or a salutory smack when required. The liberty to enter their friends' homes freely meant, of course, that our place was just as regularly invaded by the same company of noisy, often dirty, and always hungry youngsters. They could be angelic, sitting quietly while I told a story, or playing gently with Megan; but they could also be infuriating as they raced about shrieking, fighting and indulging in riotous horseplay. However, a few angry words from me or one stern glance from Neil was enough to restore order and they scattered immediately if Shirley appeared. She made no secret of her disapproval of this fraternisation, prophesying correctly that my children would learn bad language and become infested with lice. They did, of course, but these two mishaps were minor compared with the fun they had and the independence they gained.

– 4 –

'Passing Black'

As we learnt more about the poverty that surrounded us we found it hard to understand how people living in these conditions could apparently be so carefree and contented. Sounds of laughter and singing floated across from the houses in the evenings and sometimes we would see a crowd of youngsters romping and jiving in the street to the music of the mouth organs and 'clackers' – small pieces of fibro manipulated by the fingers of one hand to beat out a castanet rhythm for the dance. Small groups would gather under the trees or on the river bank, gossiping amicably for hours. No one seemed lonely or left out and even their stormiest rows seemed to blow over quickly and completely, leaving no bitter residue. They seemed to have a security and contentment the white world had lost, we decided comfortably. Perhaps they were happy with the status quo and we were worried and guilty without reason. But we were not shown the anger and frustration that lurked below the surface and as yet we had not seen these people in the context of the wider world, away from the support of this close-knit group. Out here at the Mission the prejudices of white society impinged on their lives only indirectly but how were they received when they left its sheltering confines? I soon found out for myself on the two occasions when I inadvertently 'passed black'.

The first confrontation occurred within a few days of our arrival. Megan became covered in little blistered sores that were obviously very itchy. For a day or two I rubbed on soothing lotions, bathed her in vinegar solutions and blamed the heat, the river water and the powdered milk. Then I gave up, and leaving the others with Neil, drove her to town to see the doctor. When my turn came to see him he picked up the card his receptionist had filled in and read it as he ushered me to a chair. I had given my address simply as the Aboriginal Station and the doctor smiled reassuringly as he looked up and asked pleasantly how long I had lived there.

'About a week', I replied and told him about Megan's sudden malady.

'Are you still breastfeeding her?' he asked and on hearing that she had been on the bottle for months he stood up and opened the door. Addressing his receptionist he said, 'Would you get some vitamin C tablets please and show Mrs Keating how to use them in her baby's bottle'. He turned to me and said kindly, 'Now Mrs Keating, you go out and get the tablets and I'm sure the baby will be all right in a day or two'. The interview was clearly over. I sat open-mouthed with amazement holding my fretful baby who whimpered away, completely untouched and largely ignored. The doctor continued a little impatiently, 'Go on, my dear, you'll be given something to fix up the rash. It's all right. It won't cost anything'. He stood holding the door open, a puzzled frown replacing the smile.

Then I realised why he was behaving in this perfunctory manner. He thought I was an Aborigine and this paternalistic charity was his substitute for a proper examination.

'What do you mean?' I asked indignantly. 'Whatever is wrong with my baby is certainly not caused by a lack of vitamin C. She has Pentavite in her bottle and fresh orange juice every day. She eats plenty of fruit and vegetables. How can you insinuate she is malnourished when you haven't even examined her?'

The poor man had enough presence of mind to shut the door half-way through my angry outburst. He hurried back and lifted Megan from my knee making placatory noises. He looked carefully at the sores for several minutes and turned apologetically to me.

'My goodness, I certainly made a mistake', he admitted.

'These are sand-fly bites. She must have some sort of allergic reaction. But don't worry, Mrs Keating, I can prescribe a couple of things to clear them up.'

He handed back the baby carefully and began to write. 'Tell me, Mrs Keating, what are you doing at the Mission?' he murmured.

'My husband is the new school principal', I grated, took the prescriptions and walked haughtily out. As I paid the bewildered receptionist the doctor trotted alongside whispering another apology for his unfortunate mistake. I was shaking with humiliation rather than anger. It was a new experience to be treated as one too ignorant to be consulted or questioned, but as I calmed down I realised that this was the fate of most Aborigines. It was assumed that they were uninformed and incapable, just as it was assumed that all their babies suffered from malnutrition. It took several minutes for me to realise that his apologies were most likely not for bungling the examination but for mistaking me for an Aborigine.

I found out later that this doctor was a sincere man who honestly tried to help the Aborigines. As they made up almost sixty per cent of the district's population, and many of them lived in appalling conditions, his work amongst them must have been an unceasing battle against the diseases and disorders caused by their lifestyle. His manner which seemed so perfunctory and patronising was no doubt his way of coping with the daunting task he faced each day. His attitude was common to that of many well-meaning whites. They dispensed advice and charity and expected unquestioning gratitude. They would most likely have been surprised to know that this caused almost as much resentment as the more overt forms of discrimination.

The second encounter with white authority, as seen from an Aboriginal viewpoint, occurred a few months later when Christopher was rushed to hospital and admitted to the Aboriginal section by mistake. He was nearly two years old, a sturdy independent little boy with the fair colouring and grey-blue eyes of his Scottish ancestors. The effect this episode had on him was devastating. Even now I feel guilty that I allowed it to happen because of my naive acceptance that those in the medical profession would also be socially aware and caring.

It started one Saturday morning when Neil had gone to town and the rest of us spent a couple of hours down on the river splashing and paddling in the shallows. It was a very wet, muddy and dishevelled family that started off for home about noon and as we climbed the path I announced a special treat: we would call in at the Big House and buy a bottle of lemonade for lunch. Shirley kept a store of such things for sale and this would be the first time we had bought anything from her little shop. The children were ecstatic at the thought of such an unexpected luxury and we trooped happily onto the verandah. We waited there in the cool while she went to the storeroom and I did not notice that Christopher had wandered off through the open kitchen door till I heard a strange coughing coming from that direction. I ran in just as Shirley reached him and took a half-emptied bottle of kerosene from his hands. He had seen it standing on the hearth, and no doubt thinking this was the promised lemonade, had upended it and swallowed quite a lot.

The coughing and laboured breathing became worse and I tried to pour milk down his throat but soon his eyes began to glaze and I rang the hospital. There was no immediate answer and we panicked and began to search frantically and vainly for the keys to Len's car, the only vehicle left on the Mission, as Len had gone to town in the truck. Shirley ran back to the phone and I raced out into the grounds calling for someone who could start a car without keys. Many voices answered affirmatively and several men came running. Among them was Archie the handyman who started the car while I ran to get the now unconscious Christopher. We raced towards town. About half-way along the bush track the truck appeared and Len, seeing his car speeding towards him through the dust, screeched to a halt and leapt out angrily. A few precious seconds were wasted in explanation and then the men changed vehicles and we were off again. As we gained speed Neil appeared. We stopped briefly and I gasped out a rushed account of the disaster. There was no time to change cars; I begged him to hurry home to the others who had been left abandoned and sobbing on the verandah and we both raced off. That is how Christopher happened to be admitted to the hospital by the Mission manager and how in the eyes of the hospital staff he was an Aboriginal child.

When we arrived at the hospital Len ran up the steps carrying Christopher. A sister, alerted by Shirley, was waiting and they all disappeared. I attempted to follow but I was intercepted by another nurse who steered me to a waiting room. Len returned and a little later an imposing figure in matron's garb appeared. She announced that Christopher was quite out of danger but would be kept in for observation. I burst into tears of relief and asked to see him. The matron firmly refused, stating that he was best left undisturbed as rest was most important. She added that I seemed upset, and turning to Len as she spoke, suggested that I should go straight home. He agreed and we were ushered to the door. I asked to stay until he was awake so I could explain things to him but she did not believe that would be beneficial. Her voice carried a definite note of finality and we left. I had not signed any admission forms or given any information. Len had supplied Christopher's name and a brief account of the mishap but my role had been minimal. I had no experience of hospitals except for my own forays into maternity wards and thought this was the normal routine when admitting children. Perhaps Christopher would rest better if left alone with the experts, I decided. The main thing was that he was in no danger. Everyone was delighted when we arrived home with the news. We assured the many callers that Christopher would be home in the next day or two and planned little treats for his return. I rang up that evening and was assured, that except for an inflamed throat, he was quite well. But, no, he could not come home as he needed further rest and care. I accepted that readily and asked what time I could come in to see him. Again the answer was definite: my visit would serve no purpose and would most likely disturb the child unnecessarily.

Then it started: a daily farce of ringing up and being fobbed off with the same vague assurances and the same embargo on visits. We were now convinced that some dire complication had set in and on the fifth day when the same dispassionate voice relayed the same vague message, I exploded. I demanded to speak to the matron and my desperate vehemence had the desired effect. After a few moments the matron answered. She expressed surprise at my frequent phone calls and the fact that I was allowed to use the office phone so freely. She told me my son was doing very well and that he was such a good little boy. He hadn't cried once but she was perturbed that he had not started to talk yet. I protested that he was a good talker and usually very vocal when upset.

'There must be something wrong with him,' I insisted. 'I am coming in tomorrow to see for myself.'

'Please don't upset the child, Mrs Keating. I assure you that he is quite well and happy. I will inform you when he is ready to come home.' Her voice was calm and authoritative and the click of the receiver ended the conversation.

When Neil got home that afternoon I was frantic with worry. I imagined Christopher's silent little figure sitting bewildered and lost in his strange surroundings. He had been unconscious when he was taken in and had woken to find his whole world changed — no familiar faces, a new bed in a strange big room and not even his beloved bubby blanket to console him. No wonder he was too shocked to speak or even cry.

Neil decided he'd had enough of the hospital's prevarication and rang through to the doctor at his surgery, demanding to know what was wrong with the child and why we were not allowed to visit. When the doctor heard the name 'Keating' and an angry voice protesting against his treatment, he must have had a sinking feeling of déjà-vu. When he asked for more details, he realised that once again there had been a case of mistaken identity. He apologised profusely and said he would ring the hospital immediately ordering that Christopher be made ready to go home. He said that the only reason for the prolonged hospitalisation was that the child had been admitted as an Aborigine and as such was considered to need extra attention. He would not comment on the reason why we were discouraged from visiting as hospital management was not his responsibility. When Neil reached the hospital about twenty minutes later a nurse asked him to wait, saying that the baby would be brought out as soon as possible. Neil refused and said we had already waited five days too many. He demanded his son immediately, whether dressed or not. During this angry exchange of words Christopher appeared in the corridor, a forlorn little figure in a singlet and nappy, wide-eyed and apprehensive. He had recognised Neil's voice and set out to find him. When Neil called out 'Christo' he burst into a flood of tears and started forward, his nappy falling off as he ran. Neil grabbed him and was heading for the door when a sister came in and attempted to explain. She said everything would have been different if they had known Christopher was a white child; he could have been discharged after two days. She was left standing there when Neil turned away abruptly and carried Christopher to the car.

He settled down as they drove off but remained huddled in the corner, refusing to be cajoled into any response to Neil's account of the great things planned for him. When they arrived home I ran to lift him out but he pushed away from me and turned away from his sisters and brother, ignoring their desperate efforts to comfort and amuse him. Beth came out with his bubby blanket, his cherished old shawl that had been his solace since babyhood but he threw that on the floor. He sat upright on my knee staring ahead with blank, hooded eyes, and resisted all our attempts to make him smile or speak. I was terrified that the psychological damage that he had suffered might have turned him into a mute and that he might never speak again. At last Peter grew tired of being rejected and wandered off to play. He started trundling up and down the verandah on Christopher's big plastic tractor. Christopher wriggled off my knee, ran to the door and shouted, 'My tractor'. I cried with relief as he took over his tractor and scooted off, his face intent, and eager.

The traumatic separation from his family and everything he knew and loved had serious long-term effects. He began to stammer and wet the bed, both habits affecting him for many years; he had nightmares and suffered anxiety attacks at the mention of leaving the house. It was months before he felt secure enough to believe that we would not disappear again without warning. And if Christopher suffered such traumas, so did many little Aboriginal children in the same circumstances.

The theory behind the hospital's policy may have been admirable had it been administered with sympathy and flexibility.

Many Aboriginal children had poor diets and little resistance to disease and infection, so that a prolonged stay in hospital to build them up with good food and doses of vitamins was a laudable idea. But the policy of excluding the family and refusing visiting rights more than cancelled any benefits bestowed by their largesse with food and vitamins.

The hospital staff were undoubtedly kind and efficient and the treatment given to black patients was medically correct but their policies served to further emphasise the different status of the two races. The humiliation rankled inside me for a long time and I marvel that any Aborigine who received this treatment can ever forgive the perpetrators.

We later became friends with one of the nursing sisters, Val Hand, who had just returned from working as a resident nurse on Red Indian Reserves in Canada. She was shocked to find that the Australian system was even more primitive than the North American. There at least they had trained personnel in charge of health on the reserves and the Indians were not segregated in hospitals.

Val suggested that my problems stemmed largely from the fact that I was thought to be a Mission Aborigine. They were regarded as wards of the state and the Manager was the person to be consulted in all matters. At least the town Aborigines were allowed the dignity of speaking for themselves, a small privilege but an important one when you have no other entitlements.

If I had not been thought an Aborigine I would have been allowed to stay with Christopher when he was admitted, to visit every day, and to give and receive information freely. There was no checking on his previous medical history, he was not signed in or out of the place, and though treated efficiently and kindly, was not regarded as an individual with a past or a future. He was just another little Aboriginal boy.

- 5 -
Making Friends

These brushes with authority were upsetting but were isolated incidents that contrasted greatly with the usual uneventful tenor of our lives. As the novelty wore off and our surroundings became more familiar, the excitement of the first month abated. We soon learnt to identify each house as the home of someone we knew and even the dilapidated village no longer seemed an amorphous slum.

The children were my link with the social life of the community. Soon they knew most of the people by name, had adopted the local jargon and absorbed the local folklore. They had friends of all ages — from their own playmates through to the old men and women who had so much time to sit and talk. Tales of strange creatures that haunted the river bends, descriptions of Aunt Ella's new baby and Uncle Ben's trip to hospital were all related with gusto as I bathed and fed them each night. Megan and Christopher, too young to join these daily forays, were thriving and happy. Neil was immersed in the school and enjoying its challenge. All the family were flourishing but me.

A severe dose of hepatitis the year before had left me with recurrent bouts of nausea and weakness, and these, combined with the unremitting daily grind, had taken their toll. I grew so thin, weary and worn that we decided to follow up Shirley's suggestion and get someone in to work part-time. Neil checked with the Trades and Labour Council about the hourly rate for domestic workers and we decided that we could afford to employ someone for fifteen hours a week.

I asked Shirley to recommend a girl and in due course Jeannie appeared on our doorstep. She was a sturdy girl in her mid-teens, and though I had seen her often as she strolled about with her friends, I had never met her. She introduced herself and then stood there with her head down and her face averted, ignoring my invitation to come in.

'Matron said you wanted me to start working here,' she muttered, looking anything but pleased at the prospect. I explained that I wanted her for a few hours each morning to help with the cleaning and, as she still stood in silence, I asked her whether she wanted the job. The only response was a shrug.

'Well, if you don't want it, Jeannie, just say so,' I snapped. 'I'm sure there are others who would be glad of the money.'

At that she looked up and a wide grin flashed across her face.

'Are you going to pay me, Mrs Keating?' she asked. Rather mystified I nodded and told her what the wage would be. All traces of that sullen resentment fled and her big, brown eyes shone with amusement. She listened amicably while I showed her through the house and discussed the work and then she nodded emphatically, 'Okay, I'll be here tomorrow,' she announced and was gone.

I was slightly bemused, wondering how I would cope with this girl of few words and startling mood changes. She arrived promptly next morning and set to work willingly. We worked out a satisfactory routine. Jeannie washed up and cleaned and polished while I did the beds, the babies and the washing. She kept a sharp eye on the children and they soon learnt to keep out of her way and off her wet floors. Megan was her pet and occasionally Jeannie would come back after lunch and take her for a walk to show her off to her friends.

I was relieved to find we could work in companionable silence and we soon became used to each other's presence. Our morning tea breaks were painful at first, filled with inanely polite queries and comments, but by the end of the week we had both relaxed and chattered away freely. I learned a lot about the close-knit little community and the idiosyncracies of its inhabitants. Jeannie obviously had a sharp wit and a quick, ribald tongue and I did not doubt she used both just as effectively when reporting our doings.

On the Friday of the first week she ran off happily with her pay, anxious to get to town and enjoy the fruits of her labour. On the following Monday, she was in a great mood and as she poured the tea she began to laugh.

'Peggy's real mad at me', she remarked gleefully. Peggy was her big sister who worked in the laundry at the big house.

'Oh yes, what's the matter with Peggy?' I asked.

'Well, she's cranky because I get paid and she doesn't.'

'What do you mean?' I said. 'She works for Matron doesn't she? She'd be paid for that.'

'You don't get paid for working at the Big House. No one gets paid for working on the Mission, except Archie and Mary, and now me.' She burst into a triumphant laugh and was still chuckling when Shirley appeared at the gate.

As I ushered Shirley into the lounge room I could see she was bristling with indignation. She told me that Peggy had been causing trouble, stirring up the other girls and making cheeky remarks about slave labour. Apparently it was all my fault. By paying Jeannie I had upset the whole system of requiring work in exchange for rations.

'But what about the ones who don't work?' I retorted. 'They still get rations don't they?'

Shirley swept that aside by declaring that the work was really a form of domestic training so that the girls would be fit for jobs in town and on the stations. I replied, that admirable though the system might be, I was not part of it and therefore I had a duty to pay Jeannie a full wage, as would any other employer.

'But it's more than they get in town,' Shirley answered angrily. 'Can't you see you will be making the others dissatisfied? We'd have no objection to a token payment.'

'No, I'm sorry, Shirley, but we're going to pay her the proper rate and the others will have to put up with it. Anyhow I don't think it's your business.' As I spoke I had a vision of Jeannie's family being turned away rationless and I faltered to a stop.

There was a sound from the kitchen and Shirley went across

to the door. Jeannie was standing by the table, her face blank and hostile.

'And you can go home, miss,' Shirley snapped, pointing an accusing finger.

'No.' I countered. 'She will stay until I say. I want to talk to her. And I hope there will be no repercussions for this on Jeannie or her family. If she is penalised in any way I'll report it to the authorities.'

I had no idea what authorities I was referring to, but then neither did Shirley. She turned and marched off grimly. I told Jeannie to go home and talk to her parents. If they thought it better she give up the job she was to come back and tell me, but otherwise I would see her in the morning.

She strolled back at nine the next morning, laconically remarking that her parents wanted her to stay on, and set about her work. We studiously avoided mentioning Matron, money or work practices but I gathered in time that my ominous forebodings were unjustified. News of the affair spread with great rapidity. A first-hand account of a barney between two white women was a rare addition to the Mission's fund of funny stories.

But a rift was opened between Shirley and me that never quite closed over. She ignored me completely for a week, and though she gradually relented, the former ritual of regular daily visits was never resumed. Len too lost much of his easy bonhomie, communicating with us only when necessary, and he brought back the armful of books he had borrowed. He and Shirley had decided that there was nothing to be learnt from reading them and that he would gain more from the tracts and publications sent out by his church.

Through Jeannie we began to meet more of the people. She had described them so cleverly that when they were introduced, they seemed immediately familiar and we could talk together as old friends. One name cropped up frequently in our conversation. Grandma Boney, or Kooka as Jeannie mostly called her, was evidently someone of great importance in the community. Everyone spoke of her with affection and respect and I began to regard her as some sort of tribal matriarch.

I had seen her in the distance several times, a tiny figure with shiny black skin and white hair, always accompanied by a huge wolf-hound type of dog and at least two attendants. One afternoon she passed our house on the path to the river. It was a very hot day and as she walked along she leant on the arm of one young lad, while four others, two in front and two behind, carried leafy branches to shade her. It reminded me of processions I had seen in cathedrals, but instead of a silken canopy this dignitary was sheltered by rustling green leaves. I was so astonished that I followed to watch.

When they reached the river bank the branches were stuck in the ground to form a pavilion in which she sat chatting and watching the crowd of youngsters cavorting in the river. The entourage returned later at the same steady pace. The youths, though noisily clowning and teasing each other, were as attentive as courtiers and I was considerably impressed by their devotion and by her dignity.

One morning Jeannie arrived with the news that Kooka wanted to see me that afternoon. We both panicked slightly, cancelled our ordinary routine and began preparations. I cooked while Jeannie cleaned and tidied with furious energy. She was just as relieved as I was when my cake and scones turned out well and was full of admiration for my best tea-set and tablecloth. Satisfied that all was ready she left, promising to return with Kooka about half past two. After lunch the children and I waited solemnly. Impressed by the elegance of our table setting and the unusual smartness of our attire, they behaved with a decorum suited to the occasion.

Then right on time our visitors appeared. Kooka was leaning on Jeannie's arm and accompanied by a number of women. The wolf-hound mooched along behind. At the gate the procession broke up. The women hauled the reluctant dog home and Jeannie and Kooka came inside. The children, for once overawed and silent, gazed unwaveringly at her face as we seated ourselves around the table. They knew her from their wanderings about the Mission but her great age and the aura of dignity that surrounded her evidently affected them as well.

Kooka greeted us all briefly and then she lapsed into silence.

Jeannie and I chattered nervously as we passed scones and cakes and poured the tea, but except for the occasional yes or no or thank you, Kooka ate silently. I began to think that my tea party was a complete failure but talked on valiantly. Even Megan sat mutely in her high chair and soon Jeannie too ceased speaking. I found it difficult to sustain my cheerful monologue.

Then Kooka stirred, sat back in her chair and pushed her plate aside. From her pocket she produced a short black pipe and sat holding it in her gnarled hands. Jeannie began to roll her eyes significantly towards my tobacco pouch on the mantlepiece. I quickly offered it to Kooka, suggesting that she might like to try my brand. She expertly filled the bowl, tamped it and lit up.

The children stared in amazement, drew deep breaths and opened their mouths. I forestalled the spate of questions about the pipe by handing them each a slice of cake and suggesting in meaningful tones that they should now go and play on the verandah. They obediently withdrew and I lifted Megan from her chair and placed her on a rug with her toys. But the older children moved only to the door and sat there in a semi-circle fascinated by the glow of Kooka's pipe and the thin stream of smoke that curled up from it. I rolled a cigarette and placed the tobacco and papers close to her hand.

She began to tell me how her family had been forced to move to the Mission when she was a young girl. They had been rounded up by the Aborigines Protection Board, taken from their home near Angledool and lumped together on the Reserve with more than a hundred strangers from different areas and tribal groups. I found it difficult to follow her as she spoke softly with a strong accent but she repeated the refrain 'Angledool is my home, my place' often and sadly. She was vague about dates so I guessed that this had happened many decades ago, but she still looked back on her lost home with sorrow and remembered that 'bad time'. I was very moved by her story and tried to find out why they had been taken away from the place that meant so much to her, but she just repeated the tale in a sad, sing-song chanting tone.

I have since read that remarkable book *The Two Worlds of Jimmy Barker* in which Barker tells of his own experiences as a young boy. In 1911, as part of the Board's policy to protect and educate the Aborigines, he and his family were similarly transported from their home on Milroy Station, north of Bourke, to the Mission. His description of his happy childhood years and the contrasting harshness of the regime at the Mission is heartrending and reminded me of Kooka and her sorrowful lament.

Jeannie broke the silence that followed by making a second pot of tea. Suddenly Kooka broke into another story, this one a light-hearted account of the time her people walked miles through the bush to see a train for the first time. Although they knew that this was a man-made machine and not an angry spirit reincarnated from the Dreamtime, the speed, the noise and the smoke belching from its fiery head amazed the group. They performed dances about it and one man, the singer of the tribe, composed a song in honour of the great iron snake.

'I would have loved to have heard that,' I remarked. Without warning she burst into a piercingly high-pitched chant in her own language. The four older children took to their heels and disappeared into the yard, while Megan shrieked loudly. Jeannie picked her up and went to assure the others that Kooka was not angry. Her black eyes twinkled with amusement as she finished the song.

'You didn't think I could remember the old lingo, did you?' she chuckled and proceeded to give me the English translation of each line. I was elated; I had no idea that the old tribal language still existed and yet here in my kitchen was someone who could speak it.

'Would you mind teaching me some of the language?' I asked. She nodded and patted my hand as she stood up from the table.

'I'll come back one day,' she said. 'Jeannie will tell you when.' Impulsively I picked up the tobacco and held it out to her.

'Please take this as a present from me,' I said. Kooka nodded graciously and accepted it. Leaning on Jeannie's arm, she walked to where the women were waiting. I knew I had met someone who was remarkable, not only for her great age, her dignity and wit, but because she was a witness to the last of the old tribal ways. So when Jeannie told me next morning that her grandma liked me I was more than flattered.

From then on Kooka arrived every few weeks. She always sent a message beforehand and we spent many an hour sitting over cups of tea, talking about the old days and happenings on the Mission, both past and present. Often she would sink into a comfortable silence, but just as I thought she had nodded off, she would straighten up and resume her tales.

She taught me words and phrases of the old lingo and I copied them faithfully into a large notebook, spelling them out phonetically. I used to practise these and trot out a few phrases when next she visited. Most of the time she was quite mystified and when I supplied the English translation she would laugh and shake her head. She always repeated the word until I got it right and, although I never mastered the subtleties of intonation or the new consonants required, I built up a small vocabulary and Kooka was proud of her pupil.

Unfortunately, I lost the book in one of our many subsequent moves and now I remember only a few words. The stories she told have become blurred and largely forgotten, but the memory of her earnest voice regretting the passing of the old ways is still vivid.

Kooka was saddened that each new generation was growing further away from the ways of their ancestors; they knew neither the language nor the customs of their people. One aspect particularly distressed her. She said they did not know 'their own meat'; they were eating food forbidden to them or else preparing it incorrectly. I took this to mean that each group had its own totem, an animal that was special to it, and that the younger people were violating the taboos applying to this 'meat' or totem. One of her sons knew the old law and observed it, she said, but when he died it would be lost for ever.

She spoke bitterly of the devastation caused by alcohol. The social structure of the community was being undermined by the drunkenness of so many of the men who were abdicating their roles of protector and breadwinner.

Of course, our conversations were not always on such momentous topics. We gossiped about our acquaintances, played with the children or just sat in friendly silence. The formality of the first visit disappeared; I no longer set the table so elegantly or worried about the standard of my cooking, but I always felt honoured by her visits. Even though she did not always accept, I kept up the ritual offering of tobacco as we parted. She seemed pleased to know that I would share what I had, just as her people had always done.

During the next summer she became ill and her visits eventually ceased. She was rarely seen outside, but I often got messages from her and occasionally sent her tobacco. Her friendship meant a great deal to us as it ensured that we were accepted by the people on the Mission, not just as interested, caring outsiders, but as a part of the community.

After we left the district we sent her cards and small gifts every now and then, and in the letters we received from our friends there, we would usually find the message 'Grandma Boney sends her love'. So that when a note finally arrived informing us that she had died, we felt that we had lost one of the most important and valued people we had ever known. That aristocratic old lady, with her warmth and humour, symbolises for me the best in a race we were too arrogant to learn from and too impatient to try to understand.

– 6 –
Prohibitions and Paternalism

Jeannie's coming changed many things. Not only did I gain a wider circle of acquaintances and the friendship of Kooka but I now had the luxury of spare time. I kept an hour or so free in the afternoons for the children and we swam, walked, built cubbies or just loafed. Housework no longer dominated the whole day and hours of the night. Another breakthrough came when I found a way to use my washing machine again and so ease the burden of the daily tussle with the backyard copper.

Merrita and two of her friends had moved into a flat rented out by the Country Women's Association. These flats had been built for the use of women from outlying properties who needed to spend time in town while they waited for the birth of their baby or cared for hospitalised children. The advent of four-wheel-drive vehicles and small, affordable planes had lessened the isolation and meant that the flats were not used as intensively, so that two of the rooms were let to teachers. When Merrita mentioned she had no washing machine I saw a way to solve both of our problems. My machine that had stood uselessly on our verandah was moved into the flat and I was given a key to the building so that I could come in when I wished. The girls were pleased, the C. W. A. raised no objections and I was more than happy with the arrangement.

From then on I usually drove into town once a week with the five children and a big basket of washing — towels, sheets, overalls and other heavy items. I usually managed to wash, fit in the shopping and still be back for lunch. It was a luxury to use the electric jug to make tea or coffee and to choose things from the shops instead of ordering them over the phone. The children loved shopping — to them Yarrawina was a busy metropolis and they were amazed at the size and variety of the shops, all seven or eight of them. So we all looked forward to the trips and even though I still had to do some washing every day it was a much lighter job.

We usually went in on Thursdays because that was the day the fresh fruit and vegetables arrived after a long haul from the South Australian markets. It soon became common knowledge around the Mission that I went to town on that day and I would often find someone waiting along the road outside the Mission gate. I felt guilty at first when I picked them up, remembering Len's stern words on that subject administered on our first day. I felt that I was aiding and abetting insurrection as we had been told that strict supervision of movements to and from the reserve was necessary to maintain order. But I was beginning to question the need for these anachronistic rules and was now more inclined to flout them, seeing that I was already in disgrace in the eyes of the bosses. Besides that, I knew that if I sped past, the hitch-hikers would walk to town anyway and I was condemning them to a dreary ten-mile hike.

So I usually arrived in town with the car crammed with bodies, the small ones being nursed by the big ones. The children were always pleased with the extra company and did not mind being squashed but I limited the numbers to the equivalent of three adults, not so much for safety reasons, but because I feared that a greater load would spell disaster for our small car. Those who missed out were cheerfully philosophical about it.

That was how I met Peter Doolan. I was backing the car out one morning when I became aware of someone standing by our gate. He was a tall man with a very dark face and a mane of silvery hair. The children's chorus of 'Hello Peter' was answered in an elegantly cultured voice.

'Good morning, my fine young friends. How are you all this

morning?' He smiled warmly at them and then advanced to the driver's window. 'Mrs Keating, I am Peter Doolan and I have not yet had the pleasure of meeting you. I hate to impose but I would like to get to town today. Would you be able to take me in?'

'Why certainly, Mr Doolan,' I replied and as he clambered in and settled back comfortably with Megan on his knee, I admired his style. He certainly did not seem the type to be restricted by petty rules and evidently would have scorned to wait outside the gate. He was the only passenger that day and we chatted pleasantly on the way. He told me he was on the way to see his wife, Margaret, who lived in town by the bridge. He added that many people thought their lifestyle odd, with the two of them occupying separate homes, but it suited them. Margaret had a taste for the freer life away from the Mission, while he preferred the peace and quiet of his own little house. She apparently had a habit of exploding with rage if things annoyed her and he found it safer to let her cool down from a distance.

'We seem to agree remarkably well for a short time,' he smiled, 'but then we need a holiday from each other.'

He stayed in town with her periodically and she had occasionally visited him at the Mission but a month or so earlier she had been driven into town by the Manager and told to remain there. He chuckled at the recollection. 'She did create an enormous fuss that time. I didn't envy the Manager his trip into town. But she really is a good woman,' he added. 'It's just that she likes her own way.'

By now we were at the bridge and as we dropped him off he declined the offer of a ride home, explaining that he would stay with Margaret for a few days. He thanked me, said farewell and strode off with a flourish. I wondered about Peter's background. His educated speech and courtly manners suggested that he had been one of the many Aboriginal children raised by an affluent white family and like the majority of them, he had rejected that way of life and returned to his own people. I was always glad to meet him around the Mission. His wit and poise made him an easy, relaxed companion and he always greeted us with affection, but gradually we found there was another sadder side to Peter.

One day we were in town and met him on the street. His eyes were glazed and he could hardly walk. He looked so ill that Neil approached him to see if he needed help. He staggered away and the men he had been with told Neil to let him go. He had been on the 'white lady' (a devastating mixture of metho and powdered milk) and nothing could be done for him till it wore off.

On a second occasion Neil was in town by himself and was about to walk into one of the hotels when Peter approached. He was quite coherent but had obviously been drinking. He handed Neil a ten-shilling note.

'Get me a bottle of port, Boss,' he slurred. Neil protested that he didn't think it was a good idea but Peter became angry, and pointing towards the white men drinking in the bar, he said that if Neil wouldn't help him there were others who would. And if he couldn't get port he could always buy metho himself. So Neil reluctantly took the money and returned in a few minutes with the port and about three shillings in change.

'Here Peter,' he said. 'Don't ask me to do that again. You know it's illegal. Here's your port and your change.'

'Change? What do you mean, Boss? You don't get change when you buy grog.' He tried to push the money back, but Neil managed to persuade him to keep it. Neil's account of this episode was confirmed by similar stories we heard later from both black and white sources. Though it only cost three-quarters of this amount, it appeared that the going price for supplying a bottle of 'red wine' was ten shillings. Rarely was any change given back to the Aborigines in these transactions. Apparently, some of the white community, who overwhelmingly supported the banning of liquor sales to the blacks (for their own good of course), were not adverse to making a few shillings on the side by supplying it illegally. Many publicans kept a quantity of low-grade plonk to be sold through the back door to Aborigines for a good profit. Even if they were law-abiding it could always be supplied by the many go-betweens who saw it as a way of increasing their own spending money.

The banning of liquor sales to Aborigines was based on the very evident damage inflicted by alcohol on these people. This misguided paternalism ignored the other degradations that hit them at the same time — the disease, hopelessness and ostracism that drove them to seek oblivion in drunkenness. An attempt to rectify these problems may have had some success, but this law attacked the symptom rather than the cause and its ineffectiveness was shown by the continued growth of the illegal grog trade. And if illicit, over-priced 'plonk' was unaffordable, then methylated spirits was readily available.

It was evident that prohibition on a racial basis had failed and in March 1963 the Aborigines Protection Amendment Act was passed. This allowed the majority of adult Aborigines to purchase liquor legally and to drink in hotels. Many publicans circumvented this law for years by exercising their right to bar anyone they wished from their premises, but it was a big step forward. It meant that Peter Doolan and his friends would no longer have to skulk in back alleys drinking black-market grog, but could join the rest of the community in the relative safety and comfort of the hotel where the beverages were cheaper and certainly less deadly.

Peter's drinking was confined to rare but devastating binges. He seemed quite content with his secluded existence on the Mission and his occasional domestic interludes with Margaret. I met her only once. Having heard stories of her temper and independent outlook from a number of sources I was curious to meet this overbearing termagant, who seemed the antithesis of our quiet, philosophical Peter. So I was rather pleased when Peter approached me one day in town as I was loading up the car with groceries to ask if I would give Margaret a ride home. He explained that she was not well and wanted to return to her river-bank home while he had other commitments in town.

'I don't like the thought of her walking home alone in the heat,' he murmured. 'And I would be grateful for your help.' I assured him that it would be a pleasure and he hurried off towards the park. I had just finished stowing the shopping and settling the children when he reappeared with his wife on his arm. I was amazed as they drew close. Was this tiny, demure lady the router of husbands and Mission bosses? She smiled charmingly as she was introduced and settled herself in the front seat, taking scarcely more room than a child. As we drove down the road to the river settlement I remarked that I was glad to have met her at last, having heard of her so many times through Peter.

'I bet the old rascal told you some good stories,' she chuckled. 'And how do you get on with the new Boss out there, eh?' I made some non-committal answer and as I helped her out of the car she continued, 'I don't trust any of them Welfare lot, telling you what to do all the time. I'm better off here in me little old humpy.'

It was indeed a humpy, patched with sheets of tin and fibro and leaning perilously to one side, but it was a more fitting refuge for a wild, independent spirit than the safety of the Mission with its rules and regulations.

Years after we left Yarrawina, we were thrilled to see Peter being interviewed on television. It was when the 'Freedom Riders', busloads of students and other reformers both black and white, were making headlines as they toured the country towns, drawing attention to racial inequalities. One current affairs program focused on Yarrawina and, to our delight, Peter was among the citizens interviewed. He dominated the group with his dignified presence and calm eloquence as he described the conditions under which his people lived and the difficulties placed in the way of change.

Another friend of our days on the Mission appeared one night on our television set. She was introduced as Essie Coffey, a star and producer of films and documentaries. She was shown teaching young Aborigines the bush lore of their forebears and telling them stories of the Dreamtime. I thought of Kooka and how she would have loved to have known, that not only was there a revival of interest in the old ways, but that one of her nieces was in the forefront of those encouraging the renaissance. We had known her as Essie Shillingsworth, one of the bright young women of the Mission, attractive and outgoing, with a deep, vibrant voice and an air of proud independence.

Neil met her first. He was down on the river bank one moonless night fishing in the swimming hole below our house. After a fruitless half hour he picked up his gear and moved along the path at the water's edge looking for a more profitable spot.

Suddenly the silence was shattered by a deep voice calling,

'Hey there, Mr Keating. Don't you touch my lines.' He froze in mid-step and stared into the darkness.

'Who's that?' he demanded. There was a low chuckle from higher up the bank and a figure slid down to join him.

'I'm Essie Shillingsworth,' she announced. 'And you're walking over my set lines.'

They talked for a while as she hauled in the lines, checked the bait and expertly threw out again. She recommended a fishing hole further around the bend and sure enough an hour later he had landed a big yellowbelly and two catfish. When he arrived home he told me of the encounter.

'I bet she is one of the cheeky blacks,' he added, 'I don't think she would bow down to authority. She wouldn't be afraid of God or man.'

He was right. I met Essie a few weeks later as I drove towards the gate on my usual trip to town. She was with her friend Eva and they hailed me from the shade of the tree outside the Big House. When we had completed the introductions and rearranged the seating I set off smartly, not wishing to be caught blatantly flouting the rules. I sped towards the cattle grid at the entrance to the Mission, and ignoring Neil's oft-repeated stricture to slow down for grids, sailed over it. An ominous jolting and thumping warned me that I had tempted fate once too often and now had the prophesied puncture. We all got out to survey the damage. Cursing inwardly I prepared to change the wheel. Removing the washing basket from the boot I rummaged for the jack and tools and then tried to remove the spare wheel from its niche. I struggled valiantly but it seemed to be resolutely stuck in the wheel-well. Red-faced, dusty and furious I turned to the two girls.

'It's no use, I can't budge the thing.' I panted. 'Would you watch the kids while I run back to the school and get Neil? He's going to be in a foul mood because he hates being interrupted at work and he'll rant on about speeding, but it can't be helped. This damn thing is too heavy.'

'Hey there, calm down. Mrs Keating,' Essie broke in , smiling broadly. 'Stop panicking. Anything he can do I can do better.'

She proceeded to lift out the wheel with apparent ease and in no time had changed it and was stowing things away in the boot. I was filled with admiration. Certainly she was taller and stronger than I was, but she had an air of self-sufficiency I envied. As we drove off she looked at me with a grin. 'Don't give him a chance to say "I told you so". Take the car to the garage and get the puncture fixed so he'll never know the difference.'

Then she turned and wagged an admonitory finger at the children in the back seat. 'And don't you go telling on your Mum. You don't want to hear all those grizzles about speeding, do you?'

I followed instructions and drove home with all tyres intact. Of course the story did not remain secret for long. Neil had hardly stepped inside when Peter announced solemnly, 'Essie said we were not to tell you about the tyre, Dad, so we won't.'

Some time after this Neil was in charge of the small polling booth set up at the Mission. The election issues seemed remote and unrelated to life in our isolated corner but at least the Aborigines now had a vote. The day dragged on and he was about to close up when Essie strode in alone. She got the voting papers and then stood frowning at them.

'Hell, I've forgotten which one's the Labor bloke,' she muttered. She turned back to Neil and asked. He explained that as an official he was not allowed to give advice on the candidates.

'Oh, come on, Mr Keating. Who's to know? You don't think I'll run and report you, do you?'

He was adamant. That was the law and he was sticking to it. He held out for several minutes, but she persisted good-humouredly, teasing and cajoling him until he told her.

'She is the most exasperating person,' he said as he related the story that night. 'She is absolutely determined to get her own way.'

That determination stood her in good stead. She was not content to be a shrinking violet and we followed her career with interest, from a report in the local paper or her success as a singer in a district talent quest through to her involvement in films and television shows. She married her handsome swain, Albert Coffey, and they had a large family. I don't doubt that these children grew up imbued with the same ideals and aspirations for the rights of their people that inspired Essie, and I hope they too are 'determined to get their own way'.

The casual acquaintances I made on my way to and from town were becoming friends and, with Kooka's patronage, my earlier feeling of isolation had been replaced by one of involvement in the village life. This was further strengthened when some of the women began to meet on my verandah in an informal 'sewing circle'. It became another source of contention between us and the Management, but started as an innocent attempt to solve a problem.

The Parents and Citizens Association wanted to make new curtains and other items for the infants' classroom. They asked Neil if they could use the school sewing machine that had remained unused in the storeroom for years. The machine was resurrected, found to be in excellent condition and the work proceeded merrily. But a major drawback soon became evident. As space was limited, the machine had been placed on the porch not far from his classroom and the sound of its monotonous whirr and the whispered comments of the women proved too much for his easily distracted pupils. If they sewed after school his office work was similarly disrupted.

He was relieved when the women announced they were finished and displayed their handiwork. Then one asked him if she could use the machine to make clothes for her family. Neil looked at the circle of shrewd faces all waiting eagerly for his answer and realised that this would be the first of many such requests. He hedged by expressing surprise that there was no machine supplied for their use. They told him that there was one but it was locked away and the difficulties they faced in gaining access discouraged them. The privilege was evidently granted grudgingly to those judged worthy and not extended to all and sundry. As they spoke, their enthusiasm faded and their submissive expressions suggested that they knew what the answer would be.

Neil hastened to assure them that the only problem would be to find a place to put the machine where it would be freely accessible, would not disturb anyone and yet be supervised. It was after all Departmental property and the wrath of that august body would descend on his head if he mislaid even so much as a disused sewing machine.

Suddenly the solution dawned on him and promising to talk to them in the morning he came home to present the idea to me. There was a corner of our side verandah that was sheltered and secluded, tucked away from the main living area, where the women could work in peace and my privacy would not be infringed. Then I realised that I could use the machine as well. My own small electric model sat uselessly with the other appliances still stored in their packing cases. So the next afternoon a few of the huskier boys helped Neil move the machine to its new home. It was not, as I had expected, one of the old-style treadle machines, ornate with wrought iron and fraught with traps for inexperienced sewers, but a stylish model that purred along like a dream.

The P&C were told of the new arrangements and asked to pass on the information to any other would-be dressmakers. A few days later two women arrived with their baskets of sewing materials. They were slightly diffident at first, but as they settled down to sew and I went off to iron, any awkwardness caused by the unfamiliar situation disappeared. I could hear them laughing and talking softly and when they appeared the next day with a third companion I knew the ice was broken. They were relieved to know that they did not have to ask permission each time they came but they always announced their presence by calling out a greeting as they arrived and bade me a casual goodbye on leaving.

My worst fear had been that I might be put in the position of compulsory hostess and lose the precious spare time I had to myself. That didn't eventuate and I soon felt as comfortable ducking off to read, work or rest as I did sitting with them and talking as we sewed.

Most of the sewing consisted of patching and mending, cutting up big garments to make tiny ones for the children and altering clothes so that they would last a little longer. One of the young women was a competent dressmaker and helped us all with the tricky bits like buttonholes and plackets. We pooled our reels of cotton and items such as pins and needles to save fussing about ownership and the constant rethreading of the machine and our sewing circle proceeded with surprisingly little friction.

Gradually the novelty wore off and the visits became less frequent, except for the weeks preceding a really big occasion such as a wedding. The knowledge that the machine was there and freely available was important. In a small way it symbolised the breaking down of a barrier of mistrust and we all gained an insight into how the other half lived, finding out that our similarities far outweighed the differences we had expected.

But evidently we had transgressed again. Shirley reproached the women for not using the machine supplied for them and insinuated that the use of the school machine was illegal. Len followed this up by questioning Neil's right not only to remove school property but to allow outsiders to use it. He was clearly sceptical when assured that the Education Department would agree to any measure that encouraged community participation. It appeared that the more we became involved with the Aborigines the more we offended their protectors.

One of the most respected people on the Mission was Archie Boney. He was employed as the handyman and, as an employee of the Welfare Board, had to tread a fine line between the bosses and his people. He must have been a man of integrity to have earned the respect of the former without alienating the latter, because both factions spoke of him with affection and trust. It was a responsible position involving supervision of much of the work in the grounds as well as allowing him access to the stores, the vehicles and the rest of the equipment.

He was a familiar figure driving around the reserve on his tractor, emptying garbage, supplying wood and carrying out the many repair jobs necessary to keep the ancient buildings and fences intact. Peter and Christopher were most impressed by Archie and followed literally in his footsteps. I was afraid that this reserved, hardworking fellow would regard the cluster of small boys who trailed him so faithfully as a pack of nuisances but they behaved in his presence with unusual gravity and rectitude.

They were rewarded sometimes by a ride on the tractor or in the trailer that was towed behind and on those occasions their happiness was complete. They copied Archie's every action, sitting up in solemn state and saluting me with a polite wave as they passed — after all they were not my little boys just then, they were junior handymen. For a while I was puzzled by a strange habit they developed. Peter and Christopher both began to tuck the fourth finger of the left hand under so that only one joint showed. Then one day as I was talking to Archie I noticed the two joints missing from his finger. It was their ultimate tribute to their hero.

Megan too found a 'best friend'. Jeannie had a favourite nephew of the same age and brought him down one day to visit. He was a beautiful little boy dressed in a white woollen suit and cap which set off his brown skin and shining black eyes. Megan was crawling around the floor gnawing a large bone left over from our roasted leg of lamb. She sat up watching with interest as I lifted Albert from his stroller and placed him next to her.

The two babies eyed each other warily, one clutching her bone protectively and the other clinging just as possessively to a small toy puppy. Then Albert made a lunge for the bone at the same time as Megan grabbed at his toy. Both gave affronted shrieks as they simultaneously warded off the attack and tried to purloin their rival's treasure. We separated them, found a second bone and another rubber toy and peace reigned. It was not an auspicious start but they soon began to crow and gurgle as they swam on their tummies across the polished lino, discarding the trophies that they had defended so valiantly. The older children joined in and soon the lounge room was full of laughing, sliding bodies.

Albert became a regular visitor, welcomed joyfully by the whole family and beloved by all, but acknowledged always as Megan's special friend. He was her guest at birthday parties where they sat ignoring everything but the cakes and ice-cream. They greeted each other with gurgles of happy recognition and Jeannie and I were proud as we wheeled them around in the twin pram for all to see and admire.

Then he died. Poor little Albert fell victim to one of those mysterious ailments that periodically devastated the Aboriginal infant population. It was most likely a strain of gastroenteritis to which they seemed to have little resistance. Several babies died in the district while we were there, the death toll in one town being so horrendous as to merit headlines in some city papers. That was the occasion of my final split with the Welfare Officer, Madam Gestapo, who bewailed the publishing of the grim statistics as being detrimental to the Welfare Board.

But Albert was not just a statistic. The whole of the Mission was devastated with grief. We were shattered by the tragedy that struck so suddenly and wept for the family that had lost so beautiful a child. His mother came down after a few weeks had passed. She wanted Megan to have his only toy, the little rubber puppy, to remember him by. Then she gave us a photo of him and we both dissolved into tears. I was so grateful to her but could scarcely bear the thought that in spite of her loss she still tried to comfort us. We still have the little golden dog that Megan called Syrup and the photo of Albert, dressed in his white woollen suit, his dark eyes solemn and questioning.

Albert

– 7 –
A Good Neighbour

After several months Jeannie became restive and was obviously reluctant to continue with the job. When I assured her that she did not have to stay she was quite relieved. She felt that she was missing out on the fun and excitement of life in town where her contemporaries were enjoying the teenage courtship rituals that centred round the milk bar and the open-air picture show. Happy to know that I sympathised with her need to break free from her boring life at the Mission she promised that she'd come to visit often. We saw her a few times after that, a more sophisticated Jeannie who spoke with familiarity of other towns and new ways of life.

When we met her in Yarrawina seventeen years later she greeted us with her usual friendly grin as if we'd been gone for only a few weeks. As uninhibited as ever, she hauled us on a long trek through the streets, hailing all and sundry to come and meet us. When the accompanying crowd had grown large enough to be a satisfactory audience Jeannie staged one of her slightly malicious, but amusing, practical jokes. She led us towards the hotel and gesturing for silence strode inside, her face a mask of solemn concern. She announced to her sister that 'a copper and a Welfare lady' wanted her outside. Peggy's belligerent expression as she stepped through the door, backed by a group of equally resentful and muscular friends, showed that her opinion of these officials had not mellowed and we were about to receive the brunt of her fury.

'What do you want this time?' she snarled into our faces. 'What do you bludgers reckon I've done?'

Our frantic protestations and a burst of laughter from the on-lookers stopped her in mid-flow and, recognising who we were, she hugged us heartily. She threatened to strangle Jeannie and I silently sympathised. Jeannie may have aged in years but inside that matronly exterior there still lurked a provoking teenager who delighted in mischief.

The timing of Jeannie's departure was unfortunate as I had just discovered that I was pregnant. The prospect of resuming the old dawn-to-dark workload would have dismayed me at any time, but now trying to cope with all that, as well as morning sickness and swollen feet, was too appalling to contemplate. I could hardly ask Shirley to recommend a girl and as well I dreaded the thought of those first awkward weeks of polite explanations and stilted conversations that would ensue as we became accustomed to each other. But the problem was easily solved when I mentioned it to Myrtle Green, my closest neighbour. She was a reserved woman who kept slightly aloof from the tangled web of village relationships. We met sometimes while shepherding home our children and she was always pleasant and friendly. I was surprised when she immediately asked for the job as she had seven children of her own, ranging from Dennis in his late teens to Brian who was about six. She assured me she could easily cope with the extra work as she had too much spare time now that her youngest was at school.

'My housework doesn't take long,' she said wryly. 'You can't clean these places properly. There's nothing there to clean.'

We agreed that she would start as soon as Jeannie left and so began a new era with Mrs Green taking over not only the housework but many of our worries as well. She was a most efficient cleaner and polisher; soon every surface gleamed and she gradually added extra jobs to her quota. I protested that she was doing too much, but she maintained that she liked to make things look nice and continued to whirl through the housework with skill and enthusiasm. Consequently we had time to spare and could sit talking on the sunny verandah, drinking tea, watching the children play and the village life flow past. She was from Sydney and found the Mission a strange and alien place when she moved there with her new partner, Laurie. She felt just as foreign and lost as I had been at first and was still slightly remote from the affairs of the others who, after three or more generations of inter-marrying, were mostly related. Her children adapted more easily but she could not become reconciled to the restrictions of Mission life and the wretched living conditions.

As our friendship grew Mrs Green began to tell me stories of her early life on a Government reserve on the South Coast during the reign of the old Aboriginal Protection Board. She had two sisters and their childhood years were happy, a time of fun and laughter surrounded by affectionate people. Her father's job had kept him away from home for long periods. Her mother was dead, so the children had been cared for by an aunt and uncle. But even their loving protection could not shield the girls forever and Myrtle was about seven when she became aware of the fear that hung over every family: the fear that their children could be taken away without warning or consent. Those chosen by the Board were placed with white families to be trained as domestic servants or general hands on farms. They were paid two or three shillings a week and, though housed and fed, worked a full seven days for this pittance. It was in reality a form of slave labour, thinly disguised as training, but the worst feature of the system was that these young children rarely ever rejoined their families.

When Myrtle was ten, two officers of the Protection Board arrived at the door asking to see the girls. Her uncle had been warned that a visit was imminent and, seeing the car drive into the reserve, had hurried the girls to the home of a friend who hid them. The officers insisted that the only purpose of their visit was to take the girls to Nowra to meet their father who was waiting there for them. The uncle angrily accused them of lying and vowed that these three girls would never be taken. After a fruitless search the officers left threatening to return again and again until they were successful. That night the frightened children were led out of the reserve under cover of darkness and taken deep into the bush. Their uncle made a rough shelter and remained with them that night, leaving before dawn to go to Sydney to find their father. He left food and water and begged them to stay hidden till he returned. Myrtle's voice shook when she spoke of their fear as they huddled together in the humpy, afraid of the dark, the strange noises of the bush and, most of all, of the white men who wanted to take them away.

This story horrified me. It had a happy ending for those little girls as they were taken by the father to a safe refuge in Sydney, but there were many others who did not escape as easily. And this had happened, not last century, but in my lifetime. I have seen a photo of a group of black children waiting on a country railway station in the 1940s, cowering between two white guardians. They were being taken away to enjoy the benefits of this training scheme. Sally Morgan's *My Place* and Jimmy Barker's autobiography are mere glimpses into a story of racial exploitation, terrorism and kidnapping that is still cloaked in silence.

The girls lived in Sydney after that and Myrtle was lucky that her first job was with an unusually benevolent shopkeeper, who not only paid a fair wage and gave her time off for holidays, but who paid for trips to visit her relatives. She must have been grateful that her uncle's brave defiance changed her life so fortunately. She married and had a family and lived in La Perouse until after the death of her husband when she moved with her seven children to the Mission.

Myrtle spoke wistfully of her Sydney home and all the things she missed: the 'proper house' with its washing machine and electric stove; the public transport that whisked her off to shop or to visit whenever she wished; even the breeze that blew up from the bay most afternoons in summer, cooling the house and soothing fretful tempers. The contrast with her present existence was only too evident, but she was unwilling to talk about it, warding off inquiries with the comment that grumbling wouldn't change things. Only occasionally would a chance remark reveal how hard and unremitting was the struggle to maintain her standards in that dilapidated shack that lacked even basic amenities like water and electricity. As she took home some old magazines and papers one day, Myrtle remarked that they came in handy for lighting fires after everyone had finished reading them. That was something I hadn't considered. To us paper was an essential and plentiful commodity, useful for wrapping rubbish, lining drawers and many other purposes now usurped by plastic. How did people light fires without paper, I wondered. Myrtle joked about rubbing sticks together in bark shavings, but then grew serious.

'It's the lights I miss most,' she said. 'How can you read with one little kero lamp? And how can the kids do their homework?'

I knew by now that the generator only supplied power for the official buildings and I asked how the people managed. She answered that it depended on what the families could afford. Many had kerosene lamps and lanterns, some had torches and candles as a supplement, but the really destitute had lights made from a tin of sand in which a strip of cloth soaked in fat had been placed to act as a wick. These makeshift lamps had a sickening smell and were so dim as to be almost useless, but at least they kept out the dark. The long winter nights must have been ordeals of boredom.

Just before we left I asked Mrs Green if I could see inside her house. Although the children had gone freely into all the homes, Neil and I had never been invited in. We were met outside and, no matter how friendly the greeting or how involved the conversations, remained there. Knowing that it was not a lack of hospitality but a desire to hide their destitution from strangers, we always hailed them from the gate and waited outside. But by now I felt Mrs Green and I had become close enough friends to overcome this awkwardness, so I asked her to let me see what the Government deemed suitable accommodation. She was obviously reluctant at first, but then led me over to her place. We stepped down into a dark room, the floor of which had disappeared long ago, leaving bare dirt covered by a few bags and a narrow strip of threadbare carpet. One wall was taken up by the open fireplace and a bed stood at the opposite end. Through an interior door there was a glimpse of another bed. A table and chairs stood in the centre of the room, a wash tub and bucket leaned on the wall, pots, pans and a kettle hung in the fire alcove and that was all. Everything was scrubbed and clean but even the magazine pictures stuck on the walls and the curtains tacked by the window could not dispel the drabness and gloom. I looked at the wide cracks in the ill-fitting, unlined walls and the old wooden door and I imagined the cold wind whistling through in winter. The dirt floor was swept and scrupuously clean but would be a quagmire in the rain.

Myrtle stood silently knowing that I recognised the bit of carpet and two of the chairs as ones we had thrown to the rubbish dump. I was shocked that a proud and fastidious lady had to live in this wretched shed furnished with our discards. I could find nothing to say except how sorry I was. My apology was both for my intrusion and for what she had to endure.

'Now you know why I hate this place,' she said quietly. 'It's worse than you thought, isn't it? We roast in summer and freeze in winter. No one could make it look nice.'

I went home enraged that our society allowed people to live in such conditions. I remembered the articles in the papers about the conditions in the camps that housed the post-war migrants, the indignant protests about families living in ex-army barracks, using communal washrooms and eating in communal dining rooms. There were complaints about the monotony of the food served and the general boredom of life as they waited for resettlement. The concern shown for the welfare of the new Australians was not extended to the original inhabitants. The Government provided board and lodging for both groups but, compared to the pitiful shack I'd just left, an army hut was luxurious accommodation and any Aborigine would have considered the migrants' diet to be epicurean. Anyone was welcome to share our largesse, except for those whose politics were red or whose skins were black. The migrants were screened to exclude both categories. Those native-born who fell into either group were penalised, the Menzies Government threatening to outlaw the reds, while the rest of us successfully ostracised the blacks, hoping that we could solve the problem of their existence by rejection and neglect.

With Mrs Green at the helm our cares were halved. We

appreciated her not just for her house-keeping expertise but most of all for the reassurance her friendship brought. If I was sick or tired she would take over the children; if I was upset she would listen sympathetically to my woes. I realised how invaluable she was when I had a miscarriage in the fifth month of pregnancy. Some complications occurred and a visit to the doctor turned into immediate admission to hospital. Worry about the children over-rode every other concern and the news that I would not be going home next day conjured up scenes of neglected children that rivalled Dickens at his most maudlin. When I woke next afternoon Neil was sitting by the bed. He assured me that everything was under control. The children were well and happy and he had not had to stay home from school as he had planned. Mrs Green had arrived at the house early and had taken over the breakfasts, dressed the children and bathed Megan. Two other women soon appeared, telling him not to worry as they were going to help with the chores. This continued for the next few days, leaving Neil to go to work as usual and to visit me briefly each afternoon.

One afternoon I heard the prattle of excited voices in the hospital corridor and Neil walked into the room carrying Megan with the other four following closely. They were immaculate in their best clothes, their hair brushed beautifully and their shoes polished. As they scrambled onto the bed for a cuddle I declared that they were unbelievably smart and asked Neil how he had managed it. Then I looked towards the door and there was Mrs Green, her face beaming with pride and affection. I knew she had planned this surprise and realised how lucky I was to have such a generous, selfless friend. She told me how her friends had rallied around, helping with the housework and taking the children off her hands and brushed aside my thanks by assuring me that they had all enjoyed themselves. These women bestowed their charity in such a warm, spontaneous way, extending help to those who needed it without expecting gratitude or recognition.

When I came home from the hospital on the Saturday morning a welcoming party was drawn up on the verandah to usher me into the gleaming house. Mrs Green had forewarned me that her two girls, Patsy and Robyn, were helping Anne and Beth to make it look elegant for my homecoming, so I was careful to comment effusively on everything. I praised the shining mirrors and window panes and the vases full of wild flowers and I was ecstatic about the cake they had iced but the four girls still stood waiting expectantly. Obviously there was something I had failed to admire and I looked around anxiously. Anne could no longer contain her excitement.

'Mummy, look at the doorknobs and taps,' she hinted. They were indeed worthy of admiration. The metal glowed and this time I was genuinely surprised.

'How did you get them to look like that?' I asked. Mrs Green produced a tin of Brasso from the cupboard and told me it had been among the things she brought with her when she moved to the Mission.

'I didn't know there wouldn't be any taps or doorknobs,' she smiled wryly. 'You might as well keep it over here.'

Welcoming Mrs Green as a part of the family meant getting to know her children as well and soon there was a well-worn path through the weeds that separated both houses. The older boys were naturally not interested in playing games with pre-schoolers, but often dropped in to talk cars, fishing and football with Neil. The second son, Mervyn, was due to leave school at the end of 1962 and looked forward eagerly to joining Dennis in the wider world outside the Mission. They were both handsome, independent and personable, so there seemed no reason to doubt their optimistic anticipation of better things to come. The three youngest sons, Allan, Harold and Brian, were only too happy to spend hours in our back yard organising the younger set, especially when wintery days kept them from the river. Allen took on the role of referee in football games, arbiter in disputes and general overseer, while Brian and Harold were young enough to join in the games and old enough to be always elected captains. They built billy carts and sleds and helped the girls erect and repair their cubby houses. Patsy and Robyn preferred to stay indoors with me, helping with cooking, playing with Megan and Christopher, sitting chatting by the fire and in general practising being grown-up.

Patsy was one of the super-primary (secondary school) students who was to leave school at the end of 1963. She was a bright, attractive girl with hazel eyes and long brown hair. Her position as the eldest girl in a large family made her responsible and assured, an excellent child-minder and worker but her natural vivacity often broke through. She would change from a serious young woman into a boisterous child, darting like quicksilver about the house laughing and chattering as she joined the twins in their 'dress up like ladies' game or wreaked havoc in Allan's football coaching by showing off her superior skills. In her grade was another Patsy, also due to leave school in December. Patsy Boney was tall, slim and very dark. She walked with such grace and her gestures were so elegant that we dubbed her 'The Princess'. She was rather reserved and only occasionally would her face light up with a beautiful smile that revealed the warmth underlying her usual remoteness. These two girls were intelligent and personable, possessing all the qualities needed to succeed in life, but Neil and I often wondered what fate had in store for them and whether their innate ability would be cancelled out by their minimal education.

Traditionally, most of the Aboriginal girls had worked as domestics at the hospital, in hotels or private houses in town or on the surrounding sheep stations. Scrubbing and polishing seemed to be their pre-ordained destiny, accepted by them as well as the rest of community. We were loath to see these two girls treading this well-worn path. It seemed such a waste of their intelligence and charm and we often spent hours dreaming up schemes of further education and training that would widen their choices. But isolation and the lack of money aborted each plan and, as the first months of 1963 slipped past, it seemed that Our Patsy and The Princess would soon be cleaning up after their white masters just as their black sisters had been doing since colonisation.

Then our wise and practical friend, Val Hand, who was still working at the hospital, suggested nursing as an alternative. In those days a full high-school course was not a prerequisite for nursing. They could start by working as an aide and then progress to professional training. Neil talked to the girls and they seemed interested in the career but apprehensive about working in a white environment on equal terms with white girls, while all the other Aborigines employed at the hospital occupied a separate and lower stratum. Val assured them that she would watch over them and ensure that all the staff were equally supportive. Neil spoke to a member of the hospital board who was enthusiastic about the idea seeing it as a precedent for other Aboriginal youth. We promised to help with interviews and tutor them in their studies, but it all came to naught. In the middle of the year Neil was transferred to a town at the opposite end of the state. It meant we were no longer there to encourage the girls or to walk with them into the alien white world of job applications and interviews. Val contacted them but the necessary direct support had gone and the two girls opted for the devil they knew and became domestic servants. Perhaps we could be perceived as presumptuous in trying to apply our values to these young black people but, especially in the remote country towns, there were few options open to them. It was work on the terms laid down by the white society or not at all. Self-determination was a long way off.

Later we heard about their first jobs, both on station properties. Mrs Green wrote that she was worried about Patsy, who was living in very poor conditions, and whose job not only entailed doing all the housework but also included work such as butchering and wood chopping that was usually assigned to men. Her mother eventually arranged for her to come home, but doubtless her place would have been taken by another fifteen-year-old victim. The other Pat fared much better. She was employed as a nanny and treated like one of the family, travelling with them and spending her time between the property and their Sydney home. We were told years later that she had completed a nursing course and was a Sister in a Sydney hospital. Her employers, who had recognised her talents and encouraged her to develop them, were apparently wonderful people, in direct contrast to those who exploited Patsy Green.

Mrs Green and I corresponded for a few years. She wrote about the transfer of the people from the old Mission site in 1966 to the new reserve a mile or so out of Yarrawina. She was enthusiastic about the change at first. The new houses, though small, had electricity and water laid on and so were a great improvement on the old ones, but gradually she began to sound disillusioned. The new settlement was on a barren, gravelly hill too far from the town to allow easy access by foot, but close enough to encourage the people to spend money on taxis. The children could no longer spend the summer days on the river and it was a long walk for the keenest fisherman. Boredom became the main problem and with it came an increase in its attendant troubles, drunkenness and fighting.

The new reserve was ill-conceived in that it still segregated the blacks into a small, isolated area and its proximity to town seemed to accentuate the misunderstandings and prejudices of both groups. The areas were as separate as the two sections of Berlin during the Cold War; crossing the invisible wall that kept them apart was possible but the Aborigines from the reserve came to town as outsiders, not residents, and few white people set foot in the new suburb. The problem of unemployment had not been addressed. I heard of one scheme in the late sixties in which Aborigines were employed to dig a long trench and later re-employed to fill it in. This exercise in futility was followed by several attempts to conjure up work where none existed. One plan that was mooted before we left the area may have succeeded with planning and funding by a sympathetic Government. The suggestion was that on the closure of the Mission the land should be handed to the Aborigines to be run as a co-operative farm. This was a very radical idea in that era and was firmly opposed. A useless strip of gravelly hill was chosen as their new abode.

This became known as Dodge City, a place that gained a notoriety similar to Harlem and parts of Redfern for violence and anti-social behaviour. Having known the people who moved there in 1966, I found it hard to believe the stories of degradation and brawling, but the demoralising conditions made Dodge City a ripe field for the angry unrest that arose in those first years of the movement for equal rights for blacks. The intentions behind the move were good. It made higher education, shopping facilities and health services more accessible. The people were no longer virtual subjects of the Mission manager and the paternalistic regime he represented, but unfortunately the ghetto-like locaton, the lack of employment opportunity and the absence of any social amenities largely counteracted these advantages.

Mrs Green and her family eventually moved away from Yarrawina and we lost touch with them until I saw Myrtle's photograph in *Beyond 200 Years*, an Institute of Aboriginal Studies publication marking the Bicentenary. She is shown in the lounge room of her house at La Perouse with her sister, Laura, and I was overwhelmed to see that well-loved face smiling out at me, looking much as she had done twenty-five years before. After several phone calls I found her address and wrote to her. I was afraid she would not remember me but she rang back immediately, her voice as warm and affectionate as ever. Since then I have visited her in her La Perouse home, and though Myrtle now looks frailer and smaller, her eyes still sparkle with humour and her mind is as sharp as ever. We marvelled at how swiftly the years had passed, turning us both into little old ladies. I couldn't help contrasting this meeting with my last glimpse of her as she stood in her muddy yard waving goodbye on that long-ago winter morning when we left the Mission. Now she showed me the view from her verandah, the blue water of Botany Bay shining through the fronds of two huge palm trees and, as we walked into her comfortable house, I realised how she must have suffered out there, not only because of the hardship and poverty, but also because there was no beauty to lighten the ugly drabness.

Her photo albums are full of pictures of bright, laughing youngsters, the children of those wiry little boys and girls who had romped with gusto through the Mission grounds, unaware that they were considered poor and deprived, aware only of the warmth and affection that surrounded them. These children now look out from the photo frames as assured, successful adults and Myrtle is proud of her extended family. Brian, her youngest, now a handsome man, still lives with her. He made us cups of tea and walked me to the bus stop with the innate, unselfconcious courtesy inherited from his mother. Myrtle's life has not been easy. Laurie died years ago, leaving her to bring up the children alone, but the deepest shadow was cast by the deaths of Dennis and Mervyn, those two who had looked forward so optimistically to a great fun-filled future. But there is not much time for sadness in a life so full of young people who regard their grandmother's house as their own. Lively teenagers came and went, stopping politely to listen to our talk of an era and a place that must to them have seemed incredibly remote and unreal.

Above, *Myrtle Green and Patsy*
Below, *Myrtle with Brian and Harold. Note the washing facilities*

- 8 -

A Host of Christians

Many of the women on the Mission were strong and self-reliant. They had to be, since the men either worked at jobs that entailed long absences from home or, if unable to find work, hung about the house demoralised by boredom and low self-esteem until they found some excuse for leaving. Several families had moved there because the deserted or widowed mothers had preferred to bring up their children in the safe haven of a reserve rather than face the uncertainties of life in the hostile environment outside. Except for Archie and a few others who worked on the neighbouring stations, the male population consisted of unemployed school-leavers and old men living out their retirement.

The women were the decision-makers and dominated the community in a way that contrasted markedly with the white society in those pre-feminist days of the early 'sixties, where the image of the fragile little woman protected by the powerful male was idealised in every women's magazine. Equal pay was still a topic of bitter dispute, married women were not encouraged to work and pregnancy meant resignation from a job in most cases. Men's role was to lead; women's to support and follow. So it was a surprise to find the accepted order overturned in this backwater and women running the affairs of the community.

Neil discovered this when his Parents and Citizens Association met at the school. In our previous experience all of the office-bearers in these bodies had been men, even if women did most of the practical work. This group was a female enclave and he was surprised at its strength. He wondered how it would function in a community with such meagre resources. The usual role of these associations was to act as a channel for communicating with parents and eliciting their support educationally, but also as a means of supplying finance for school projects and supplementing the meagre resources supplied by the Government. Fundraising in such a poor community seemed a wild improbability and Neil concentrated successfully on developing the group into a forum where everyone felt free to express opinions and ask questions. He deliberately refrained from suggesting schemes that required finance but inevitably the topic of funding arose. The women were not perturbed, stating that if Neil could get his hands on some tobacco, they could easily raise a considerable amount of money by raffling it in town. Eight packets were donated by obliging shopkeepers. This was the first of many such projects and they were proud of their success in supplying the school with extras.

The ladies proved to be as resourceful and supportive in every aspect of school life, tackling problems of behaviour and hygiene with the same calm practicality. They dealt with lice, ringworm, truancy and bad language; they knew which families needed gentle persuasion and which ones needed an ultimatum. Neil's first appointment had been to a genteel school in a North Shore suburb of Sydney. He remembered the matters that had concerned the parents and staff there and the enthusiasm with which solutions were sought. The problems at the Mission could not have been more dissimilar, but both groups showed the same tenacity in working for the betterment of their children.

It was just as well the women were so stalwart, as the destruction of their society had affected the men severely, leaving them a minimal part to play. They were no longer the protectors of the tribe and those who could not obtain work were deprived of their image as providers of food and shelter. But even more demoralising was the loss of their most important role as custodians of the spiritual life of the people, the sacred beliefs that had been handed down through each generation since the

Dreamtime. Aboriginal life had been governed by strict laws that ensured survival and these were based on an intense spirituality. Perhaps the worst crime of the white conquerors was to denigrate these beliefs and enforce their version of religion so suddenly and ruthlessly. The take-over of sacred sites, the destruction of sacred objects, and the derisive dismissal of their ancient faith left a hopeless despair that could sometimes only be forgotten in drink.

With their old beliefs ousted, the Aborigines sought to replace them with Christianity and so fill the terrible vacuum that existed. Their whole ethos had been centred on their land; every rock and hill had been significant in that spiritual web that bound them to the earth. Now they had been driven off these sites by the followers of this new and powerful God. They had nowhere to turn for solace but to the churches who spoke of love and acceptance and held out the promise of a new Dreamtime in heaven to their followers. But the multiplicity of creeds was bewildering to those who had once had such a clear vision of their duties and destinies. Instead of one voice pointing out the way, they were besieged by representatives of many sects, each claiming to be the sole purveyor of the truth. This was evident at the Mission and, after more than a century of diverse preaching, confusion was still rife.

Well-meaning clergy frequently descended upon us with almost identical messages under different brand names. The services were held in the community hall and were well attended. There were a few true believers in each sect, but there were also many who attended each service impartially. A minister who played a guitar or an accordian drew a good crowd as did those who gave out fruit and sweets. Most were welcome as entertainment, a break in the monotony of Mission life. Special occasions like baptisms or First Communions were celebrated enthusiastically. A party was always laid on, goodies were provided by generous parishioners from town, and everyone rolled up.

The first of these celebrations occurred a few weeks after we arrived. One of the Methodist Sisters, a hard-working and pleasant young woman who combined social work and spiritual guidance in a most efficient manner, had called to meet me. She mentioned that she was preparing two of the Mission girls for their formal acceptance into the church. These two were well known for their wild, unorthodox behaviour and I was suitably impressed at her ability to convert such unlikely candidates. We watched the happy event from afar. The girls were escorted to the service by a large crowd and the singing and laughter attested to the success of the party that followed.

Several months later a member of the Anglican Bush Brotherhood announced the same good tidings about the same two girls, and in due course we watched the newly Anglicised sisters and their friends being treated to a similar celebration. Then early the next year the Catholic priest told us that he had converted the girls to his faith, baptising them during the school holidays. When I told him of their previous conversions he looked rather crestfallen but then smiled ruefully.

'Well, it can't hurt them. Besides giving them an each way bet on the right path to heaven, it means they get a good party every few months.'

Most of the clergy were tolerantly aware that the same people turned up at every service and participated in the rites of each denomination. They seemed to share the ecumenical feelings of the congregation and to accept that their services inspired conviviality rather than reverence. I met most of them, especially the regulars who lived in town, as they occasionally dropped in for tea and sympathy during their pastoral visits. They were varied and interesting characters. All spoke of their anxiety to help right the injustices that confronted them daily, but they seemed overwhelmed by the enormity of the task. Social justice was not a big issue in the churches at that time; charity to the poor and unfortunate was stressed, but this was mostly interpreted as donating money to alleviate their suffering, not altering the system that caused it.

It was not long after our arrival that we met the first and most memorable of these ministers. He was the Catholic chaplain to the Western Aborigines but had been given the job of administering the local parish for three months while the usual priest was on holidays. We were both shocked by the scenes of poverty and deprivation that surrounded us, on the Mission and on the fringes of town, and so had much to talk about. He knew the people from both places and was glad of a sympathetic audience, while I was delighted to act as acolyte. Father Kileen was a gentle man with grey hair and a worn, tanned face dominated by the Irish blue of his eyes. His voice retained a lilting brogue, especially when he warmed to his favourite subject, the problems faced by the Aborigines, and the white attitudes that caused those problems.

Despite his unworldly appearance, Father Kileen was practical and realistic, rejecting the 'noble savage' theorists who wished to return all Aborigines to the wilderness remote from white society; except for a few areas in the deserts of the centre, no wildernesses were readily available. The tribes who lived there were not likely to welcome an influx of urbanised Aborigines from the eastern states. This solution was a hundred years too late and he rather suspected that some of its proponents saw these arcadian enclaves as picturesque tourist attractions. He attacked the paternalism practised by the Welfare Board, private charities and the churches. The genetic assimilation which aimed for the gradual absorbtion of the blacks into the white community was dismissed as a type of genocide which would impoverish the country as a whole. All through our long discussions he returned continually to one point: when the Aborigines gained true equality, they would overcome their difficulties and emerge as a strong part of the nation, but the whites must be prepared to pay heavy restitution for past injustice. Money must be poured into health and education services to achieve that equality and a constant campaign against racial injustice must be initiated and enforced. That view was radical and unpopular in those days, but he practised what he preached and thereby provoked a lot of hostility.

Father Kileen's devotion to his black friends amounted almost to an obsession. He spent every spare moment with them and had visited and stayed at even the most remote camps. This unorthodox behaviour met with a mixed reception from his white parishioners. On one of my rare trips to Mass in town I met a woman who told me that he was most unpopular as he was neglecting his pastoral duties by spending too much time out on the reserves.

'He actually cuts their hair, using his own combs and scissors,' she whispered angrily. 'Then he comes back here and conducts our services. You know how lousy they are. I can hardly bring myself to go to confession; I feel all itchy at the thought of it.'

She apparently did not mind her minister teaching those people as long as he refrained from touching them. Another faction supported him, but feared that this constant ministry to his beloved outcasts was not only absorbing most of his meagre stipend but also undermining his health. He did seem to grow thinner and wearier each week.

I used to watch him wandering about the Mission visiting the people in their houses or talking earnestly to the youngsters who congregated under the big peppercorn tree. Sometimes he would join the group on the riverbank watching the children who splashed and cavorted in the swimming hole. He would sit unselfconsciously on the bank, his bony, bare feet dangling in the water and his black clerical suit becoming streaked and spotted with mud. It was usually covered with a film of dust and a confetti of cigarette ash and hours of yarning over open fires had imbued it with a strong smell of wood smoke. Often he would call in for a talk and a cup of tea. Once when I gave him a large cooked meal instead of the sandwich he usually had, he was unable to eat more than a third of it. He explained that he was not used to banquets and without embarrassment he borrowed a container and took the rest home to eat next day.

He was a born story-teller and, for all his saintly ascetic appearance, he had a wild sense of humour. His tales of the people he had known and the strange places he had visited were all the better for the slight exaggerations that spiced them and I loved to watch the laughter sweep across his craggy face. He was in charge of the parish for only a short time before he returned to his roving apostolate, and I was left to mourn the loss of this unique friend. We liked his replacement, a young cleric who dressed informally, mixed well with the Aborigines and was deservedly popular, but Father Kileen was a hard act to follow.

He is still remembered by many western Kooris with affection and reverence.

The Catholic services at the hall were an eye-opener to one used to the formality of the old Latin Mass where the congregation listened in silence as the priest intoned the elegant, archaic prayers, the only interruptions being the soft responses of the altar boys, the tinkle of a small bell and the disciplined voices of a choir. The hall was full when I arrived that first Sunday and Father Kileen was already at the altar, pouring out a stream of Irish-accented Latin. The congregation was moving about happily, chatting, admiring babies and calling greetings to late-comers. Children ran around and the general din was punctuated by a shriek from one or a burst of laughter from another. My arrival was noted with surprised approval and a further exchange of greetings ensued. They followed the usual format of the service, standing and kneeling in the proper places, so someone was obviously familiar with the ritual and I gradually worked out which of them were practising members of the faith and which ones were there for the entertainment. They all listened intently to the brief sermon, nodding approval and murmuring agreement occasionally. Then the words of dismissal sounded and the real socialising began. Father Kileen always joined them in the hall after he had packed away his vestments and spent the next hour or so listening to their troubles or sharing their joys. Sometimes there was a box of oranges or a bag of lollies to be shared but even if there were no goodies there was always a sympathetic ear for those who needed it.

When the new priest came he decided to bring a little law and order to the proceedings and to initiate some audience participation. He arrived at our place with a grand plan. Having discovered that I knew the Latin responses usually spoken by the altar boys, he gave me the job of answering the responses and acting as overseer to the two boys he intended to train as assistants. I was to prompt them and tell them when it was time to perform their duties. In addition I was to instruct the congregation by explaining what was happening at the altar.

I was not at all enthusiastic but the young priest's eagerness to encourage participation by the laity swept all objections aside. He went off to instruct the two lads while I searched for my old Missal to brush up my Latin. News of this innovation had been mooted abroad and a large crowd turned up for the next service. They watched with interest as the two embarrassed boys and I took up our positions at the front and the priest explained what we were to do. With a flourish he turned to the altar and began the service. The silence was broken by a gasp of astonishment as I rattled off the first response and this was followed by muffled giggles as we continued. They had never really heard the words of the service and here were two familiar people standing up before them chattering away to each other in a most incomprehensible language. When I turned and explained the next part of the Mass they seemed relieved that I spoke in English. They nodded politely and murmured 'Yes, Mrs Keating' occasionally, but then I was off again intoning that strange gibberish, my face crimsoning as the titters increased.

Then it was the boys' turn. A small bowl of water and a starched white hand towel stood on a small table beside us and I handed them to the boys. They had practised this, but as I prodded them forward they cast an agonised look at their audience and froze. Then one pushed the bowl back into my hands, dropped to a squatting position and hid his face. The other bolted for the door, flinging the towel aside as he ran. A moment of silence was followed by a crescendo of startled comments and then a gale of laughter swept the congregation. The priest stepped over to retrieve the bowl and the towel.

'Carry on,' he whispered. 'Tell them what comes next.' Scarlet with embarrassment I faltered out a few sentences but we had lost our audience this time and I stopped. The laughter and amused speculation got louder and the priest turned again.

'Ask them to be quiet,' he ordered.

'How can I?' I retorted angrily. 'They can't hear me and I can't hear you. Let's forget about the responses.' He started to grin.

'Well, what about ringing the bell for me anyhow?' I grabbed it and shook it with such enraged vigour that the noise stopped dramatically. Each time it rang from then on all murmuring ceased and at the end of the service one old lady bent towards me, 'You did a real good job, Mrs Keating. I never heard anyone ring the bell as good as you,' she said consolingly.

Thus ended my job as chief acolyte and the young priest's effort to train up some altar boys. He had much more success with a few rousing hymns and the services continued in their old familiar form but perhaps there was a diminution in the noise level. That was not due to my bell ringing, but rather to his habit of stopping and glaring at any group who exceeded an acceptable volume. As the culprits were usually teenage boys who had encountered him in the impromptu football games he organised or girls who were rather impressed by his muscular good looks, his disciplinary efforts were not resented. On the contrary his popularity grew and he became a minor cult figure for the younger generation.

The good-humoured, inattentive crowd that filled the extra seats at the Catholic Masses patronised the other denominations as well. Without the disadvantage of a service conducted in Latin, the rival ministers most likely coped fairly well, although most had a few rueful tales of occasions when moments of solemnity turned into hilarious farce through misunderstanding. Each church conducted a service perhaps once a month and all were held in the same hall, so it was understandable that many of the floating congregation had forgotten to which particular brand of Christianity they owed allegiance. In essence it was quite an ecumenical community.

I met many of the clergy who visited the Mission and admired most of them. Among them were the Anglican Bush Brothers, members of a religious society formed last century to cater for the needs of isolated communities in the Australian outback. I knew little of its history except that its members, recruited mainly from English universities, signed up for a minimum of three years and lived during that time under strict rules that included poverty and celibacy. I had an image of idealistic young Englishmen, suffering the rigours of this outpost of the Empire, enduring their stint of martyrdom in order to earn the reward of a parish in the leafy English countryside. So I waited with some trepidation to meet these paragons and remembered all those curates whose rather effete virtues had been portrayed by so many writers from Jane Austen to Agatha Christie.

The two young men who drove up one day and introduced themselves as Brother Paul and Brother Andrew were a big surprise. They were two ordinary, good-natured Australians who roared with laughter when I told them what I had expected. They were certainly not delicate souls and really enjoyed their ministry, even though it entailed living on a stipend of £120 a year, frugal pocket money for any young fellow even in 1962. Their living expenses were paid by the Brotherhood's headquarters in Dubbo, but their pay of a little over £2 per week ensured a life of monastic simplicity. The founder of the Australian Bush Brothers, Frederick Campion, was an aristocratic visionary and his colleague, Charles Matthews, was a socialist who horrified the western establishment by speaking on the platform at a Labour rally in the 1906 elections. Any lingering suspicions that I may have retained about a bunch of stuffy clerics was further dispelled when I learnt that one of the early recruits, Brother Alf Clinton, had marched with the striking shearers to block the train load of strike-breakers on their way to Brewarrina in 1930. The movement attracted men with diverse opinions on every topic, united only by their devotion to the Brotherhood. Our two new acquaintances certainly followed an interesting tradition and, though conditions in the west were no longer so uncivilised, they showed a similar zeal and dedication. But, as in the early days, there was still a great diversity in the personalities of those who formed the Brotherhood. Inevitably one arrived who was startlingly different and whose presence gave rise to many amusing stories and much malicious laughter.

He came from England and stood out like a visitor from another planet in this district where skin colourings ranged from the faded terracotta of the whites to shining black, and people spoke in an almost uniform laconic drawl. He was plump and very fair, his voice was clipped and high-pitched and his elision of the consonant 'r', as well as his fruity vowels, made his speech as alien as Latin to his Mission flock.

Sensibly, he always wore a large straw hat, but his choice of tight white shorts and long white socks was not so felicitous, accentuating as they did his rotund form and rather mincing walk. His strange voice and near albino colouring were enough to attract attention but, combined with a self-assured pomposity of manner, he was an inevitable target for nicknames and parody.

One afternoon I watched him haranguing a group of youths who were lounging beneath a shady tree. Brother Richard had an aversion to idleness and I did not doubt he was exhorting them to bestir themselves, to 'play the game' or whatever cliché he favoured at that moment. After several minutes he trotted off to his car and as it drove away one of the boys stood up. He strutted out to face the others and began a cruel parody. His gestures were perfect and I would have loved to have heard his version of the lecture, as the audience rolled on the ground with laughter. Then the lad gave an airy salute, turned and minced off, with one hand clutching an imaginary straw hat, while the other fluttered in the air at shoulder height. His long brown legs aped a knock-kneed gait and his bottom twitched exaggeratedly from side to side. It was great acting and for a moment I could really believe that the boy's long brown body had turned into a short fat one.

My unseemly amusement was increased by the fact that I had just endured the good Brother's monologue on 'the white man's burden'. I had never been a Kipling fan and disliked having to listen to a defence of the British Empire couched in his gung-ho terms.

The reserves was often visited by the Pastors of the Aboriginal Inland Mission. Surrounded by their friends and followers, they naturally had no reason to drop in for tea and a gossip as did their white counterparts, so I did not meet them. I noticed however that they were treated with respect and affection by all the people and when I was eventually introduced to Pastor Duncan Ferguson I realised why. The Aborigines trusted him for he was one of them; he understood their problems as no white man could and the respect shown to him by the wider community must have been a boost to their self-esteem. I was most impressed. He exuded dignity and though we talked of trivialities such as the weather, the children and my impressions of the district, his eyes shone with interest and understanding. I could see why he was always welcomed so warmly, not just as a minister but as a real leader of his people.

One morning I watched a crowd leave the hall and follow the path to the river bank. They disappeared from view and soon the sound of singing drifted up. I could not resist any longer and slipped through our back fence to a vantage point overlooking that part of the river. I could see people gathered on the bank singing a hymn while they watched a small group standing in the water before a white-clad pastor. He had his hands on the head of a young man and was evidently conducting a baptismal ceremony. It was a dramatic scene with the brightly clad group standing out vividly against the shining brown water. It reminded me of a picture of Christ being baptised by his cousin John in the waters of the Jordan. Here were the same dark-complexioned people gathered to watch, and there was even a hawk circling in the sky in place of the artist's symbolic dove. I was struck by the aptness of the setting, both artistically and historically, but realised that I could be regarded as a prying intruder and left.

People who are deprived and degraded seek the only solace available, the promise of better things to come in another life; the wonderful spirituals, the religious songs of the American Negroes, came out of slavery. The people at the Mission were searching for a creed that would compensate for their lowly position in society. A group met regularly in a house with a battery wireless to listen avidly to the Radio Church of God, evidently finding comfort in messages relayed across the Pacific in the unctuous voice of a fundamentalist preacher. Some people were lucky and found a religion that satisfied them, but it must have been hard to reconcile the message of brotherly love preached by the ministers with the way they were shunned by the rest of the Christian community. A black person in a white church was a rare sight in any town I had ever visited.

– 9 –

Rations and Bush Tucker

While the churches were eager to supply spiritual succour to the Mission dwellers, no one seemed anxious to improve their physical conditions. It took us some time to realise that these were even worse than we had first thought. We could see that the houses were shocking and most people were shabbily clothed, but we believed that the Government would supply plenty of nutritious food. After all, this was the lucky country — a cornucopia of natural products that were sent to all parts of the world. Surely no one could be hungry here. We found that although there was no starvation and the rations supplied were enough to stave off hunger, they were dull, unappetising and lacking in nutrition.

I began to notice how avidly the visiting children watched when I prepared our meals. The smell of roasting meat would draw a crowd of eager helpers and there were always volunteers to scrape out the mixing bowls or finish off any left-over corners of pastry or cake. That was quite normal behaviour for any child and I thought nothing of it until the day I saw one of the older girls beckoning her two little brothers to join her outside. Behind her back she held a newspaper parcel. I had just put it in the bin and knew it contained the meat and vegetables my children had left on their plates. She carefully divided the scraps into three portions and in a few seconds the paper was back in the bin and the children resumed their game in front of the lounge-room fire.

Then I was in a dilemma. I couldn't feed them all but I hated to see their eyes fastened intently on the food that I dished up for the children, or worse still, on the left-overs they had rejected. It was not the troop of pre-school urchins that were the problem. They lined up unselfconsciously for snacks during the day but were always collected at meal times. Some of the older children visited me regularly in the evenings and they were the ones that gave most concern. They liked to help as I bathed and fed my five offspring. This desire to help was most likely sparked off by the chance to try out something novel. They could lounge in a chair before the open fire reading magazines or listening to the radio, play with the rubber toys that floated in a bath wastefully full of hot water or sit in the kitchen helping feed the babies while the savoury smell of cooking floated in the air. I was loath to send them home, especially when the cold autumn afternoons curtailed their outdoor activities. To most people our living area would have been considered spartan and shabby, but to these children it was luxurious in its warmth, light and space, as was the amount and variety of food we ate.

We never solved that problem. If there were only a few present I could offer them something but I could not play Lady Bountiful to a large crowd. They were not hungry for bread or damper; that had been their staple diet since birth, but even the shyest would accept a spicy rissole, a strip of bacon or a 'chewer', my children's favourite treat — a chunk cut from the outside of a roast, crisp and crackly and dripping with juice. Cheese, honey and dried fruit were all exotic tastes, as were most of the sauces and flavourings we took for granted. Many had sampled only a few of the more common fruits and vegetables and these were rare treats rather than everyday foods.

The rations were given out in carefully measured portions according to the number in each family. For weeks I watched the women trudging back home on ration days and wondered what they had in their bulging sugar bags. Shirley assured me that there was more than enough to ensure a healthy, balanced diet. Bread and meat were handed out every few days; flour, tea, sugar, potatoes, jam and powdered milk were supplied once a week and basic groceries like salt and baking powder were given when needed. That sounded reasonable enough, especially if supplemented by fruit and vegetables grown on the Mission. But then one of the women showed me her portion. The meat was mutton flaps, a cut with a minute amount of lean meat hidden among masses of fat and bone. The potatoes would have lasted two days, and when I asked about the fruit and vegetables she laughed.

'I've heard that tale too, Mrs Keating,' she said. 'But I've never seen the vegies or the garden either.'

There had once been a large garden fenced off for that purpose but now there was only a small patch that supplied the Manager's needs. Fruit, vegetables, eggs and cheese were not regarded as necessary everyday fare, but rather as luxuries too rarified for the unfortunate indigents. The paltry, monotonous diet was designed merely to keep people alive, and it must have been a bitter struggle eking out the provisions to ensure they lasted until the next ration day. Sometimes they ran out, of course, and a great deal of borrowing and bartering went on to alleviate this. I heard that babies drank sweetened black tea in their bottles in place of milk. A crust of bread dipped in tea was commonly used as a pacifier.

A Mothercraft nurse would have been horrified at the diet given to the babies and toddlers, but there was none around to advise or reprimand the young mothers. Shirley was the sole authority and she was apparently satisfied that all was well. My opinion of her expertise plummeted further when I heard her refuse extra potatoes on the grounds that they had little food value. The wonder was not that many infants died but that so many survived this regime. The school children were better off as they were supplied with a peanut butter or vegemite sandwich and a glass of powdered milk at recess. The families that depended solely on the rations would have had trouble enough satisfying their children's hunger without worrying about abstract notions like nutrition.

When money was available everyone enjoyed small treats. The children had sweets and cordials, the adults smoked cigarettes, went to the pictures or took taxis from town. This did not happen often, but when it did it aroused the righteous wrath of their critics. The Aborigines were seen as spendthrift and profligate, lacking the white man's virtues of saving and foresight. It was true that they lacked our desire to store up possessions and money, and that their tradition of sharing was in direct conflict with the white man's desire to hoard, but it is always easier to save when a goal is achievable. The Mission dwellers could never save enough to buy a comfortable lifestyle and the desire for some frivolous touch of luxury, even one as insignificant as a lolly or a taxi ride, is common to all those who face a life of dreary poverty. The same charges are levelled today at the 'dole bludgers' by those insensitive souls who regard the 'waste of taxpayer's money' as the paramount sin.

The rations were not handed out to all and sundry. Recipients had to have no other means of support, hardship had to be proved — and pity help the family whose breadwinner spent his wages on the way home from the shearing shed. Our dismay at the inadequacies of the handouts was increased when we learnt that those who received them had to work at any job the Manager stipulated. These rations were paltry payment for even the lightest labour, and an improvement in their quality would most likely have ensured a more willing work force.

Fortunately the Aborigines had other means of augmenting their food supplies because of the favourable siting of the Mission. It was on the banks of an abundant river and was surrounded by bush. Here they could use the remnants of their old hunting skills and, even though game was relatively scarce, enough could be found to add variety and quality to their diet. The river yielded fish, mussels and freshwater turtles and occasionally water birds were snared. Wild duck and even black swan was a palatable change from mutton flaps. There were kangaroos, emus and wild pigs in the bush, but catching them was not easy. Fishing lines, nets and snares could be made or bought cheaply, but for these larger animals guns were needed.

Len sometimes went hunting with the men and shot a kangaroo or emu to be shared out among the people. As Neil had a small .22 calibre rifle he was invited along and rather reluctantly he accepted. Having grown up on a coastal farm, he had often shot rabbits, foxes and other vermin, but he had never regarded our national symbols as fair game. However, this was necessity, not sport, and he climbed into the truck aware that all eyes were on this newcomer, doubtful of his chances with the small rifle and even more dubious about the ability of a 'schoolie' to shoot at all. A kangaroo was sighted and he was offered first shot. He brought it down with a shot through the hip and finished it off quickly. The Aborigines were delighted and Neil's standing in the village was enhanced.

His first emu came much later. On one occasion Len refused to go shooting or allow the men to use the truck, so they approached Neil seeing that he owned a trailer as well as a rifle. Once again he was successful and they returned with a huge bird. As it was unloaded, the men told Neil they could still catch their quarry in the old way. Half the party would spread out, encircling the bird, driving it towards a group who lay hidden in the long grass with knives and clubs. These men then sprang up and battered the emu to death. No one could use spears or boomerangs, guns were not available and so this inefficient procedure had to suffice unless someone came to their aid.

'That's bloody hard work, though,' said one. 'And its even harder walking back home carrying the bloody thing on your back.'

This may have been one of the tales they told the gullible whites but I do know that they ran down young pigs in the bush. These were taken home and fattened for slaughter. The piglets were penned up and fed on scraps and some species of plants. One rusty-red weed growing near the Mission was pointed out as suitable pig food and I don't doubt there were others. The pork had a strong, gamey taste but would have been an epicurean delight after a steady diet of mutton flaps.

The larger animals were either butchered and the meat shared out among the families or a communal feast was prepared. Emus were always cooked in pits, thrown in whole, feathers and all, covered with earth and roasted slowly over the coals in this giant cooker. The pits had been dug on a pleasant stretch of grassy riverbank upstream from the Mission and we knew when a feast was imminent because of the increased activity on the river path. The whole procedure took hours from the initial gathering of sufficient wood to ensure a massive bed of coals until the bird was eventually unearthed, its outer skin discarded and the succulent flesh carved. These parties were immensely popular and were perhaps one of the customs remaining from the old tribal life. Neil and I did not ever sample emu but he always knew when it was on the menu. Its pungent smell, exuding from the pores of so many sweaty little bodies, filled the classroom like an almost palpable cloud.

Perhaps because Neil helped with the hunting, or more likely because they were naturally generous, the Aborigines often shared their catches with us. Someone would appear on the doorstop with emu eggs or freshly caught fish and hand them over casually, brushing aside my gratitude with an embarrassed smile. One afternoon when I was given a parcel of pork chops I remembered those warnings about the 'bludging blacks' who would always be sponging off us. The reverse was true; the gifts were given with a natural grace and had no strings attached.

My first emu eggs gave me pause. They were so enormous and so beautiful with their dark blue-green shells that I was reluctant to break them. The first one I made into scrambled eggs, ending up with a huge orange mass, enough to feed two families. The second one I beat into a cake mixture that called for three eggs and watched with dismay as it rose mightily, overflowing the cake tins and oozing across the oven. I learnt that they were equal to about nine hen eggs and with the aid of this arithmetical equation I could handle them easily.

One gift we jettisoned in the dark of the night. It was when I was pregnant and subject to frequent bouts of nausea, so to be given a parcel which once unwrapped revealed a lump of shining, dark red meat quivering on the stained paper, caused my stomach to contract ominously.

'Mum thought you'd like to try a bit of swan,' the boy murmured and I managed to stammer out my grateful thanks before I bolted for the back yard. When I returned he had gone and I felt as miserable about offending him as I did at the thought of eating such a beautiful bird. I had to lie to the boy and his mother when I visited them the next day to thank them for their gift. I did not have to explain my hasty exit as they, together with the rest of the Mission inhabitants, had already guessed that I was pregnant. I assured them that I had enjoyed the casseroled swan that I had prepared the night before. Not even our own children realised that a mundane steak and kidney mixture had been substituted for the breast of swan. Neil had secretly consigned it to the river under cover of darkness where it was undoubtedly welcomed by the yabbies and other scavengers. He rather regretted that we would never know whether we had missed a gourmet dish and I had to admit the absurdity of spurning the meat of one species while chopping up the kidney of another with equanimity. But we were relieved that most of the offerings we received were of a less exotic variety.

We were not offered anything as unusual as snake but many a fine reptile ended up on the Aborigines' dinner tables, if the boasting of the children were to be believed. We had learnt to take many of the tales they told us with a grain of salt but snakes were very plentiful and were supposedly delicious, so there was no reason to doubt the truth of this story. All the school children, even the younger ones claimed to be able to kill a snake with ease. We knew that it was not a difficult feat if you possessed a large, strong stick, or a golf club or a garden hoe, but there was a definite shortage of any such implements on the Mission. The sticks that litter the ground out there are small and brittle, not substantial enough to kill a snake in the usual manner. One day however, Neil was shown how to kill a snake western-style. He was down by the river one afternoon when Bunna, one of the older school boys, neatly and efficiently disposed of a large snake that was lying motionless on the path. The boy gathered up a handful of small, chunky bits of wood and bending down, he sent the first stick whistling just over the reptile. It reared up angrily and the next missile hit it squarely near the head. It collapsed stunned and Bunna walked up to finish it off with a final blow. Holding up the still twitching body, he grinned at Neil.

'You see Sir, you got to make 'em sit up so you got a target to hit. They always do it. Then you knock 'em out with a smack in the chops.' He carried the snake up the bank and threw it on the nearest ant hill.

Snakes loomed large in our lives. They seemed to be everywhere and it was just as well that none of us had a snake phobia. In the summer they could be seen through the missing floorboards of the verandah as they sheltered under the house from the fierce sun. They sought out cool spots by the river and under the tank stand and if disturbed would slither across the bare ground to disappear in the cracks that had opened up in the baked earth. In early spring we found them sunning themselves on the paths or any warm surfaces. Snakes are reputedly more aggressive in that season and it was in spring that we had our first snake drama.

One Saturday after lunch I was preparing Megan for her afternoon sleep. I had sponged her grubby little body and left her sitting on her pottie on the laundry path while I went inside for a change of clothes. She was by now an independent, active toddler and I could hear her singing contentedly to herself. Suddenly the lilt of the nursery rhyme gave way to a scared wail of 'booey booey', a term she had begun to apply to ants and other little crawly insects. So I was not concerned and called out, 'Don't worry, Megan. They won't hurt you.'

The frightened chant rose higher and I stepped on to the verandah to see what was causing the fuss. A large brown snake was gliding along the path. It stopped in a patch of sun about a yard from her feet. For a moment Megan, the snake and I froze in a silent tableau. Then I gasped out a warning to Neil who leapt from the kitchen in one stride, grabbing up the snake stick as he went. The vibration of his steps alerted the snake, and rearing up, it turned to face him in one fluid movement. He cracked down with the heavy stick and killed it. We were both trembling with shock as we saw how close it lay to our baby's feet. She was more surprised and interested than afraid, but now I understood the revulsion and terror that has usually marked man's relations with this creature.

Only one other snake was unfortunate enough to inspire fear and thus meet a sudden end at our hands. This hapless little reptile was lurking in our woodheap one dark night when, with the children in bed and Neil down fishing, I decided to ease the aches and pains of my pregnant body with a long soak in a hot bath. I gathered up bath salts, oils and a good book and prepared to light the heater. But the chip box was empty and I had no option but to plod wearily out to the woodheap to replenish it. Not bothering with a torch or a container, I bent over and began to scoop handfuls of wood chips into my apron, holding it out by the hem to form a receptacle. I straightened up and then felt one of the bits of wood begin to dance vigorously and frantically around in my makeshift container. I was paralysed with fear as I realised what it was that was wriggling and leaping so close to my stomach. My first idiotic thought was *If I drop it, I'll lose all my chips*. And was followed by *If I drop it, it will bite me on the foot*. So I stood like a statue, clutching the bunched-up apron with its cargo of precious chips and one enraged little snake. A flash of torch light from the river path jolted me from my frozen trance and I called, 'Hurry, Neil, hurry. I've got a snake in my apron.' He broke into a run, no doubt thinking that I had finally gone round the bend.

'Drop it. Let it go,' he shouted as his torch focused on my burden and then, grabbing the apron, he sent its contents flying to the ground. With one whack he dispatched the poor terrified snake and held it up. It was a complete stranger to us, a pretty slate-grey creature about two feet long with a shiny black cap. No one at the Mission or in town could identify it, so we sent it to the Sydney Museum and found that it was a harmless nocturnal snake. I regretted its unnecessary death, but Neil was more amazed by my reluctance to drop my collection of chips. Only a weary, pregnant Mum would understand my aversion to wasting even the smallest effort.

As a keen fisherman Neil soon got to know the river. He found the favoured spots for collecting mussels and worms for bait and located the deep holes that provided the best fishing. He also found that the mosquitos out west were larger and hungrier than the coastal breed. One evening on one of his earlier outings he met Mervyn Green on the path to the river.

'You going fishing, Sir?' Mervyn asked. 'You won't stop down there long tonight.'

Neil thought the boy was referring to the huge, ghostly 'dog' that was reputed to haunt the stretch of river called the Woolwash and assured him that he was not afraid of bunyips.

Mervyn laughed. 'No Sir, the dog won't get you but the mossies sure will. You won't stop long.'

He was right. Even dressed in combination overalls, thick socks and a balaclava you needed layers of insect repellant and grim determination to last for more than an hour on a summer night. But with the dedication of a true fisherman Neil persevered, escaping to the river when the burdens of school work and the propinquity of his boisterous family proved too much. There too he got to know the men and youths of the village. They also fished zealously, both to provide food for their families and to enjoy what was perhaps their only legitimate pastime. Mervyn and his stepfather, Laurie, were keen fishermen and soon invited Neil to join them for a day at their favourite spot far upstream. It was a long walk but the hole lived up to its reputation and the three of them were soon hauling in nice fish. About noon Laurie suggested lunch and produced from his pocket a small packet containing salt. He cleaned and filleted three unscaled yellowbelly and placed them scale-side down on a wire grid over the coals. He thickly salted the skinless side of the fillets and, after a few minutes, flipped them over. The salt and oil from the fish dripped off into the fire leaving the fish perfectly seasoned and with a delicate smoky flavour. He cut three plates from the bark of a nearby tree and served up his gourmet dish. Eaten with fingers, it was an ideal meal — delicious food, no fuss, no mess, no washing up, and an idyllic setting.

We often enjoyed fish cooked this way on our picnics, although we substituted plastic plates for Laurie's more picturesque bark variety. These outings were our only family recreation and on most fine weekends we would drive to one of our favourite spots on the river bank. There were no fences on the surrounding stations and rough bush tracks led to the good fishing holes where we could swim, fish or just loaf under the great gum trees. We discovered billabongs where we waded barefoot among the reeds and water lilies, feeling in the mud for the hard shells of the big oval mussels. The children slid down mud banks, climbed trees, gathered wild flowers and crept silently down the bush paths as we attempted to stalk kangaroos and emus. Occasionally we found an emu's nest and one day we were rewarded by the sight of a male emu striding along followed by a clutch of beautiful, stripey chicks. Kangaroos thudded away as we approached, but the other bush dwellers, the birds, insects and lizards seemed unconcerned by our presence as we shared their stretch of the river bank. No picnic day is ever a complete idyll. At least one child would get stung by a wasp, fall from a tree, slip in the mud or tangle a fishing line, but these were minor mishaps and we always drove home reluctantly. As we passed the sad little houses in the bleak compound and saw the people lounging there I often thought our day had been spent enjoying those things that once had been part of their daily life. The Aborigines had been forced to exchange the untrammelled freedom of the bush for these meagre trappings of the white man's way of life without any of its privileges.

The river was the focus of most activity in the summer months and its proximity made life bearable. Besides being a source of food, it was the main social centre and the paths that led to the water were well-trodden by all the people who sought refuge from those unlined, sun-baked houses. They swam, paddled or just gossiped in the cooler air under the river gums. The young and active swung from ropes tied to the over-hanging branches or fought mock battles in their make-shift tin canoes. The hours spent sweltering in the hot school must have seemed endless to the older children who no doubt envied the freedom of their younger siblings. These youngsters were learning lessons as valuable as any taught to their elders. They learnt to swim, climb, fish and throw missiles with deadly accuracy but more importantly they developed the imagination and ingenuity that is often stifled by too many toys and structured entertainments.

Our own children exulted in this carefree existence and learnt skills that would not have been developed in a more sheltered town environment. Peter, a natural athlete, soon gained fame for his prowess in most physical activities. He could throw a stone with devastating accuracy, play football, climb and fight, but his real love was fishing. At four he could handle a line or rod with ease and was even more of a fishing fanatic than his father. His greatest hour came when he caught an eight-pound catfish. Neil had taken him fishing one afternoon to a spot a few minutes' walk upstream from the Mission. They fished fruitlessly for half an hour and Neil decided to move to a new position around a shallow bend, leaving Peter perched on a low mud bank, his eyes fixed on the line that he had thrown towards an old sunken log on the other side of the pool. Neil had just settled himself comfortably when he heard sounds of a scuffle. Then Peter called out anxiously, 'Dad, hurry up. I can't hold him'. Neil raced back to see Peter being pulled slowly but surely into the water, both hands grasping the line as he slipped down the muddy bank. A big catfish had swallowed the bait and was intent on reaching the safety of the log, while Peter was just as intent on preventing it. The fish was tiring as Neil arrived, hauled his son from the river and helped him land the monster. It was almost as big as Peter, but he insisted on carrying it back home immediately. Neil cleaned the fish and attached it through the gills to a stick so that Peter could carry it over his shoulder Dick Whittington style.

A few of his friends joined him as he staggered up the last rise towards the house and, alerted by their excited babble, I looked out to see Peter, exhausted and muddy but with a smile of pure joy lighting his face. The tail of the fish trailed in the dirt, but he resisted all efforts of help until he was able to lay his trophy proudly at my feet. After we had duly admired the fish he set off on a tour of the Mission, determined that everyone should witness his triumph. He was greeted with much acclaim and assured by the elders that he now held the record for the biggest catfish caught on the Mission. This episode firmly reinforced Peter's long-held opinion that he was indeed living in the best place in the world.

- 10 -

Trouble on the Mission

The Australians we had known before coming to the Mission were mainly descendents of the early British and Irish settlers: laconic types who hid their emotions and discouraged open displays of joy, sorrow or fear. White people like us kept their anger damped down to smoulder inside in long silences, and expressed their disapproval in measured, dignified tones. The Aborigines on the other hand could go straight from smiling placidity to boiling anger that exploded in a fearful slanging match and reverted as quickly to cool equanimity. It was as though a volcano erupted and then died away leaving no trace of the fiery outburst. During the angry flare up, words flew like weapons between the protagonists. The voice tone changed from its usual low, husky timbre into a hard, high-pitched metallic monotone. The message conveyed was secondary to the harshness of the words, as insults were hurled repeatedly and meaninglessly.

When I first heard this, the hair rose on the nape of my neck and I feared a terrible physical outcome, so deadly and unforgiving were the words and tone. But to my surprise it suddenly ceased and the adversaries walked away peacefully. This verbal warfare was mainly confined to disputes among themselves. Only occasionally was it directed towards those in authority, and then mainly only after much provocation. Harassment by whites was usually met by a frozen silence, by downcast eyes and averted faces. Doubtless this particular behaviour pattern had become ingrained in the early days of settlement when white bosses had wielded a gun or a whip with impunity if faced with any resistance.

Both of these ways of reacting were often evident in school. Neil worked out that it was better to ignore the noisy outburst if possible, especially when it occurred in the playground; his intervention only served to drive the fracas underground and so prolong it. It would continue in any case till both sides had rid themselves of their grievances. The stubborn retreat into silence that occurred when a child felt that he had failed in some way or had been shamed by those in authority was better dealt with by leaving the sufferer alone. A few sympathetic words whispered unobtrusively helped, but the uplifting lecture, the rallying jollity and, worst of all, the sarcastic remarks sometimes used by teachers to stir their charges 'out of the sulks' had the opposite effect. It was not surprising that Aboriginal children dropped out of school at the first opportunity.

Living on the edge of this community, I had time and opportunity to indulge my insatiable curiosity. I spent much time during those first few months staring across the Mission from my perch on its outskirts and thus noticed an intriguing phenomenon. The apparent contentment and easy camaraderie that had so impressed me in the summer began to fray as autumn set in. The people went about their daily routine with their usual placidity and greeted us warmly when we met, but I couldn't help feeling that they were hiding a deep anger. Groups stood about muttering and gesticulating, but fell silent as we approached. There was a definite air of resentment and disaffection and we worried that our family may have been the target of this real but intangible ill-will. But the children continued to enjoy as much care and affection as ever and I never felt personally rebuffed, so we put it down to a case of an over-fertile imagination.

One evening we noticed someone signalling with both arms like a tic-tac man at the races. He was hidden from the main buildings by an old pepper tree and seemed to be relaying a message to a group across the common. One of them in turn signalled towards the furthest houses. Then they all disappeared. A few minutes later we saw several men moving among the trees towards the river path and concluded that they were off to town via the short cut across the river. Then a few days later Neil reported seeing the mysterious summoning of a group who gathered in the bush at the back of the Mission. On the third occasion I became so overcome with curiosity that I asked Shirley what was happening and why everyone seemed so discontented.

To my surprise she burst out with an angry tirade against the 'troublemakers who were undermining Len's authority'. The feeling that by joining with the white authorities Len had betrayed his own people had grown into real resentment. He was met by open disparagement and rejection. The dissident group was led by two brothers whose status amongst the other residents was high enough to ensure a loyal band of followers. Ray and Laurie were tough colourful characters who earned good money when they wished and consequently felt no need to kowtow to the Welfare Board. Having been born on the Mission, they regard it as their rightful home and not only ignored the rules but defied any threat of eviction. Faced with such a challenge to his authority Len had no option but to crack down hard on any infringements of the rules and so the antagonism grew. Even from our position on the outskirts of the community we had sensed this unrest.

Shirley illustrated the extent of the troubles with the story of the raft. The Aborigines had built this themselves and it was a handsome contraption, a wooden platform supported by several oil drums lashed together. It was propelled across the river by pulling on a strong overhead rope that was attached to a tree on either bank. A second system of ropes ensured that it would not break loose and could be anchored to either side of the river. Len had seemed quite proud of the ingenuity of the builders and had even supplied them with materials from the storeroom.

The growing antagonism had changed all that goodwill. Len had retaliated against what he saw as a passive disobedience campaign by refusing all lifts to town except for official visits and emergencies. He then decided to further restrict access by destroying the raft, thus eliminating the short cut through the bush. This meant that those who wanted to socialise in town were faced with a ten-mile trek by the road, unless of course they could hitch a ride with the occasional passing vehicle. So one night he cut the rope and set the raft adrift. It floated downstream and there was only the sight of the severed overhead rope trailing in the current to remind everyone that those who lived on the Mission did so on the Manager's terms.

Shirley related this saga with a triumphant air, but I could not share her conclusion that the miscreants had learnt a lesson and the troubles would cease. The resentment had grown to a miasma that permeated the whole community so that even we Keatings could feel it, unaware though we were of the real issues or the identity of those Shirley referred to as troublemakers. I mentioned it to Father Kileen and to my surprise he stated that the people's unhappiness and anger had grown to become a disturbing force.

'Something is brewing and unless it is damped down the resentment will boil over. And of course, being so vulnerable, the Aborigines will come off second best.'

He then asked if I was scared. I laughed at the idea and assured him that we had nothing to fear. Everyone was friendly and as the anger was not directed at us, we were completely unaffected by any ruckus on the Mission.

'That's partly right, Patsy. These people would not willingly hurt anyone, let alone you and your family. But if a person is pushed beyond his limits he will strike out. It will be white authority he is attacking, not individuals, and you and Neil are white. You are not one of them. Just don't get in the way if trouble boils over.'

As he left he added that I had never seen an explosion of rage like an outburst from an angry Aborigine. 'It's like these western storms,' he murmured, looking out at the purple cloud bank piling up on the horizon. 'It blows up dramatically, makes a hell of a noise and then disappears as quickly. But it can cause damage. Don't forget that my girl.'

Not long after this a minor boil-over occurred which gave credence to his little lecture. Shirley had called in with a message and was sitting at the kitchen table. Through the open door I saw Laurie turn in at our front gate and stroll up the path.

He stopped for a moment to chat with the children who were playing in the yard and then greeted me cheerfully.

'Good day, Missus. Where's the Boss?' he asked. 'Thought he might like a spot of fishing tonight. I've got the bait and it looks like a good night for a cod or two.'

'He should be home any minute, Laurie,' I answered. 'Why don't you sit down and wait?'

He stepped onto the verandah and was about to reach for a chair when he saw Shirley. Her face was a mask of contemptuous dislike and the cheerful grin disappeared instantly from his. She stood and announced that she would come back later.

'Why, Missus, don't you like my company?' Laurie drawled softly.

'Don't speak unless you're spoken to,' she snapped. 'You've got no right on this reserve anyhow.'

'This is my bloody home, you fat white cow.' He grated out the words in a clipped, hard tone. Shirley began to rave in a shrill, venomous voice.

'Get out. Get out of this house. Go back to your own place immediately. The Manager will hear about this. Get out.'

'No, Missus, you can't put me out of this house. This is Mrs Keating's house and she's not telling me to go.'

'I have every right. This is Welfare Board property and I'm in charge here and I'm telling you to go.'

By now both had lost control. Shirley's face was crimson and she was almost incoherent as she pointed dramatically at the gate and reiterated her threats of vengeance if he did not leave immediately. Laurie was quieter but his voice was deadly as he described Shirley, her husband and the whole Welfare Board in decidedly improper tones, to the delight of a small crowd who had gathered outside the gate. My children were standing open-mouthed and wide-eyed a few feet away. I attempted to break in on the argument several times but neither protagonist was in the mood to listen. Then I grabbed up the snake stick and banged it loudly on the verandah table.

'Stop,' I ordered in a voice that had quelled many a noisy

playground melee. 'You are both wrong. You can't put Laurie out of my place, Shirley, because while I pay rent here I say who comes and goes. And I'm shocked at that language in front of my children, Laurie. The Matron can't order you out but I'm asking you to leave until she goes.'

For a moment there was silence. Laurie turned towards me, his eyes still slitted in anger. Then he shook his head slightly and blinked his eyes as if to get things in focus. Gradually his face was transformed by a grin. He bowed towards me.

'My apologies, Mrs Keating. If you ask me to go I certainly will,' he said and turned to stroll down the path to the gate. 'I'll come back later if I may.'

I began to usher Shirley out through the side door to avoid another confrontation. She was obviously upset and I started to murmur a few consolatory words, but she brushed me aside with a comment on the undesirable types that were ruining the Mission, leaving me in no doubt that the description applied to me as well as to Laurie. This was confirmed next day when a girl appeared at the door asking that I return the petrol iron Shirley had lent me. I had offered to return it when we sent back the borrowed refrigerator, but had been assured then that there was no need as there were others still lying unused on the storeroom shelves. This sudden request was a clear signal that cordial relations between the two families had once again ceased.

Len reinforced that later with a formal visit to complain of a cubby-house built by our children and their friends. It had been erected around a corner post and it was indeed, as he charged, protruding onto Welfare Board ground. We were to remove the cubby as it made the place look untidy, he stated. Biting back the obvious remark that it was scarcely less attractive than the houses supplied by that body, we agreed to do so. Then came the real reason for his visit. He warned that he was considering reporting us for 'transporting liquor' into the reserve for the Aborigines' use. We were astounded at this because we had been very careful to observe the rules pertaining to alcohol, knowing that the ban on Aboriginal drinking was still valid and that it was rigidly enforced on Government reserves. Neil had carefully refrained from offering a beer even to fishing mates like Laurie and Ray, even though he knew they both drank openly in town.

When asked for proof, Len announced that we had been seen giving Mission residents lifts to and from town. He had noted that these people often carried shopping bags, parcels and cardboard cartons with them when returning in our car. He asked if we ever searched these containers and, if not, how could we be sure there was no liquor brought in. We replied that naturally we had never pried into our passengers' possessions and regarded such behaviour as a gross invasion of their privacy. Len then blustered that we were being used as dupes. Liquor could be smuggled in, hidden in the grocery bags or even tied beneath the car body and we were breaking the law by not checking. This paranoia was not worth answering and Neil told him to go ahead and report.

So began weeks of non-communication, with the two families ostentatiously avoiding each other, much to the glee of the other residents. An open declaration of hostilities was made when the men were ordered to stop supplying us with firewood as had been customary hitherto. Everyone noticed as the trailer lumbered deliberately past our woodheap and we were greeted with ironic cheers when we returned to the Mission the next weekend with our own supply. Then the embargo was extended to include the rest of the community. No one was to be supplied with wood except the old and infirm and, of course, the big house. This was a serious matter now that winter had set in, as the bush close by had long since been denuded of anything suitable for burning. So the men asked Neil to help out with his car and trailer again and their weekly expeditions must have been further proof to Len of actively seditious behaviour on our part.

Tensions mounted as the restrictions grew. There were no rides to town, no wood supplies and visitors were strictly vetted. To make matters worse the cold weather meant that social gatherings by the river were curtailed and people huddled indoors. Boredom and irksome confinement caused the rumbles of discontent to grow louder. Angry quarrels flared up and bitter insults were hurled. Mutterings against the Boss grew more open and one night we heard a derisive shout of 'You want to watch yourself Shiney-eye' float back from a figure passing the office gate. That term cropped up again and Neil asked what it meant.

'You know those long, crawly things with mean, shiney eyes and poison fangs? Those nasty buggers that bite you when you're not looking? Well, that's what this Boss has turned out to be,' Laurie answered. 'A bloody snake in the grass.'

So the hard core of antagonism grew. By now we knew who the 'troublemakers' were and it surprised us that they got away with such outright derision. It would have been a brave welfare officer who attempted to evict Ray, Laurie and his mates. Most of the families, including our own, were not drastically effected by Len's restrictions or the rebellious mutterings they engendered. We were too busy with the chores of family life. We cooked, cleaned and cared for children. People visited, told stories and gossiped and I was enjoying the new friends I'd made. The seditious behaviour we glimpsed merely added a bit of spice and Neil and I forgot our earlier fears of a dramatic outburst. Then one night we were taken by surprise.

We were reading by the kitchen fire, drinking coffee and enjoying the warmth and peace. It was after nine o'clock and our lights were the only ones still shining. The little houses across the empty common were dark and silent. Then faintly from the furthest street came random sounds, a few snatches of angry words, a banging door and the excited barking of a dog. We took little notice but then the words became a chant, an eerie thread of sound rising and falling in unvaried rhythm. Other voices began to call out and one dog after another joined in a chorus of barks and howls until there was a wash of sound forming a background to that strange, insistent monologue. Realising that this was no ordinary domestic row, we slipped out into the yard and stared into the darkness of the common.

A dim light was shed by a thin curve of moon that slipped in and out of the clouds. The houses stood black against the paler sky but lights suddenly flickered and doors opened. Figures began to move across the intervening spaces and in one clearing a group appeared. It moved erratically, fanning out behind a tall figure and that figure seemed to be the focus of all the furore. We recognised Ray, unmistakable even in the faint light as he towered above the others. He strode along, one arm punching out a message of defiance towards the sky, beating out the rhythm of his chant 'Shiney-eye, Shiney-eye, I'm going to get you, Shiney-eye.' His voice was unrecognisable, high, nasal and metallic. A hubbub of sound rose and fell around him. The murmur of anxious voices, the wailing of a child and sudden, hysterical shouts of laughter were all dominated by that grim threnody.

Then the sound of movement stopped. Ray broke from the crowd and moved slowly towards the big house. He disappeared into the blackness of the tree-shrouded garden, but his voice could still be heard, softer now but even more menacing: 'Shiney-eye, Shiney-eye, I'm going to get you, Shiney-eye.' We stood open-mouthed, shocked into silence by the unreal drama of the scene.

'I think I'd better go and see what's happening,' Neil began, but then our side gate banged and we heard running footsteps on the path. My heart lurched with fear as we turned back towards the house. Shirley burst through the screen door into the kitchen, young Steven in her arms and Caroline clutching at her long, woolly nightie. We ran inside. Shirley was gasping with fear and exhaustion and the children were wide-eyed with shock.

'You've got to help,' she panted. 'That Ray's gone mad. He wants to kill Len.'

Neil helped her into a chair as I took the children. 'Where's Len?' Neil asked. 'And what's Ray doing?'

She managed to stammer out that Len had locked himself in the office and was ringing the police. She had been too afraid to stay alone in the house with the children while Ray rampaged along the verandahs, shaking at the doors and windows, kicking and swearing as he kept up his threatening chant.

'Len has loaded his rifle,' she faltered. 'Someone will get killed.'

Neil turned and ran into our bedroom, returning with his rifle. As he loaded it, I recoiled in horror.

'You're not going to shoot Ray?' I whispered.

'Don't be crazy, Pat,' he snapped. 'I'm going to talk to him. He's quietened down a bit but I want to get him away before the police come. If he sees that Sergeant Brownridge he'll start raving again. Someone will get hurt and it will most likely be Ray.'

He checked the rifle and passed it to me. 'You take this. If Ray saw Shirley coming over here he might think Len came with her. If he tries to come in, order him to stop and let him see the rifle. If he won't stop, shoot in the air.'

Aghast at the prospect, I began to argue but brushing aside my objections, Neil ran off. I gingerly stowed the rifle in the farthest corner and turned to Shirley who was sitting by the table with her head on her arms.

'We are going to have a cup of tea whether you like it or not,' I asserted. 'Help me with the kids while the kettle boils.'

She raised her tear-stained face and actually managed to smile at the two children. We fed them with warm milk and biscuits and, as they refused to leave the kitchen, we tucked them up with blankets and pillows, turned off the light and began our vigil. She told me of her nightmare journey through the dark garden with the children clinging petrified to her hands, conscious all the time that Ray was snarling and prowling on the verandah a few yards away. As they reached the common, she had grabbed up Steven, and clutching Caroline, had run madly towards our kitchen light. Her soft slippers were studded with burrs and she bathed her wounded feet as we sat in the firelight drinking the strong tea. I dutifully kept my eyes on the window, conscious all the time of the rifle standing against the wall behind me and hoping desperately that no one would cross the common and enter our gate. I mentally rehearsed versions of 'Who goes there?' but they all sounded artificial and pompous and I was greatly relieved when Neil's familiar outline loomed up.

He assured Shirley that all was well, Ray had gone back to his place and the Mission was quiet again. He escorted her back to her house, carrying the sleeping Steven while Shirley flapped along in a pair of Neil's sandshoes holding Caroline by the hand.

Neil returned and collapsed into his chair. I poured him the last of our brandy and he told me the story of his adventure. When he left the house and started across the common he had been aware of little groups of apprehensive watchers but ran on till he reached the shadow of the big tree by the office gate. He stopped there to gain his bearings. He could hear Ray's angry mutterings and worked out that he was prowling around the verandah near the office door. Reluctantly Neil stepped from the comforting darkness and started up the path. Suddenly three women darted out from the shadows and grabbed him firmly by the arms.

A voice hissed in his ear. 'What do you think you're doing, Mr Keating?' and he was dragged back into the shadow of the tree. He recognised one of the young mothers, a slight, shy girl whose apparent fragility was belied by the firmness of her grip. An older woman repeated the question.

'I'm going to talk to Ray,' Neil answered. 'The police will be here soon. I'm going to get him to come with me.'

'He won't listen to you. Don't go near him. Do you want to get belted up?'

'He won't touch me. He's a friend of mine,' Neil objected.

The older woman spoke. 'That won't make no difference. He'll just see a white man and that'll be enough. He'll go for you. Leave this to us, Mr Keating. We'll get him.'

The women walked slowly up the path, not attempting to hide, calling to Ray in soft, coaxing voices. They disappeared onto the verandah. Gradually the angry muttering stopped and the only sound was that soothing chorus. Neil waited anxiously, his heart still thudding from the fright of his sudden arrest by the women. Then he saw four figures descending the steps. Ray's arm was held by the older woman and she spoke calmly and casually about a nice cup of tea at her place. Ray answered and the menace had gone from his voice. The watchers melted away as the group crossed the common and disappeared into one of the houses. The crisis was over. Neil left the shelter of the tree and started off for home. As he neared the gate, he saw a woman's figure emerge from under our tank stand and run swiftly down the path and off into the darkness. He halted, bemused at this new development in the night's unreal drama. A voice chuckled close by and one of the men caught up, telling him not to worry. The fugitive was one of Ray's family who had earlier received the first blast of his anger and had wisely sought out this remote and unlikely hiding place.

Neil then received a brief account of the first stage of the episode and its immediate origin. It appeared that Ray had arrived back on the Mission that night after a few weeks' work on an out-lying station. He was full of good cheer from his celebrations in town and eager to renew his acquaintance with an attractive young woman who had recently moved to the Mission. He sprang from the taxi and entered her house only to find it deserted. She had gone. Inflamed by disappointment and rage, Ray accused his family of driving her away. Prudently they fled to the neighbours who in turn felt the brunt of his anger. Sensibly they too got out of his way and, alone and frustrated, Ray turned his fury onto his old enemy, the Boss. Perhaps he figured that Len had been finally responsible for his girlfriend's banishment, or more likely, he seized on this opportunity for the showdown he had been seeking for weeks.

Whatever the reasons for the outbreak, it provided us with a juicy topic to discuss as we brewed up coffee and toasted our legs in front of the stove. Presently we heard the sound of a car approaching and watched it draw to a stop in front of the office. Two policemen alighted and went inside. After several minutes they returned to the car and as it drove across the Mission its lights swept in an arc across the dark houses where hidden people watched as avidly as we did. It stopped in front of a house, a large figure got out and stepped into the full glare of the headlights. We gave a sigh of relief as we recognised the Crown Sergeant, a man noted for his liberality and a great contrast to his colleague, Brownridge, the established adversary of all Aborigines and Ray's particular foe.

He called out, 'Are you there Ray? Come on, mate. Don't keep me waiting. It's cold out here.'

There was a moment of silence and then the door opened. Ray strolled out calmly and they both got into the car and drove off. It was as though the curtain had fallen on a tense drama and we, the audience, turned and went quietly off to bed. That night seemed to marked the end of the troubles as well — the eruption acting as a catharsis, draining away much of the bitterness and ill-feeling. For some time the atmosphere lightened and life settled down. The wood was delivered to all the houses, including ours, and the gubby truck once more carried passengers to town. Cordial relations were resumed between our two families, although in a much more formal manner. The rest of the year passed with only occasional visible signs of underlying resentment. Ray no doubt received due punishment for his attack on his masters, but the whole incident was soon submerged in the usual daily struggle to keep afloat in the morass of poverty. 'The winter of our discontent' soon gave way to bright, brief spring. Things never seem so bad when it's warm and sunny.

Megan in the front yard

- 11 -
The Black Soil Track

One aspect of the life in the west that cannot be ignored is the weather. Its moods and contrasts are great. The freezing nights of winter give way to the burning summer days with only a brief pause for the mild perfection of spring. Months of drought with the sunsets luridly crimsoned by the dust that obliterates the horizon are interspersed by spells of rain that turn the ground into a squelching sheet of mud. Dust storms can blacken the sky at midday, causing the fowls to hurry to their roosts, while housewives quail at the very thought of the aftermath: the hours of shovelling out and sweeping up the dust that infiltrates every crack. But it was the rain that dominated our lives more than any other phenomenon. It came rarely but when it did it made a spectacular entrance and often threw us into turmoil.

We had been there about a fortnight when the first storm came. The sky had been cloudless and by early afternoon the heat was so intense that the children and I lay on the cool lino in the hallway hoping to catch a stray breeze from the river. They were almost asleep as I droned on about the interminable adventures of the three little pigs when we were aroused by a strange drumming sound. I went out onto the verandah to see a wall of low, black cloud and an opaque curtain of rain heading towards us from the south. A storm was about to hit and I dashed towards the clothes that flapped wildly on the line, then remembering the boxes of books still unpacked on the verandah,

I leapt back shouting, 'Inside, everyone, it's going to rain.' The children, already over-awed by the approaching noise, interpreted my haste as panic about the storm and ran shrieking wildly after me as I heaved and tossed the boxes towards the door. The first great drops thundered onto the roof, the baby woke and screamed and in one minute I was sopping wet as I frantically shoved the children and the cartons to safety. The din of the rain on the iron roof was deafening and I strained to shout above it, attempting to assure the children that there was no need to be afraid, that I loved storms and we needed the rain. They were clearly sceptical of my explanation of why rain sounded noisier here than in our old house and were vastly relieved when the storm passed just as swiftly, leaving pools of water steaming in the yard. For a long time after that they regarded rain clouds with apprehension and reacted to any storm with great excitement.

This sense of exhilaration was increased by the narrow escapes we had when we were in town shopping. When the black soil roads became wet they changed rapidly from being merely slippery to that stage where the mud forms a glutinous mass clogging the wheels and making progress impossible. As the summer storms came up so quickly, we experienced many a dramatic escape from disaster. On several occasions our shopping expeditions were interrupted by the warning that storm clouds were approaching. Helped by the shop-keepers and friendly bystanders, those who had to leave the built-up gravel roads would hurriedly load up their vehicles and begin a thrilling exciting race against the lowering clouds. Very early in our stay Neil performed the virtuoso feat of skidding off into the brimming table drain and charging through the water at speed, dodging bushes and trees before regaining the dubious safety of the road. The children were elated at this performance and later when we returned to the region of bitumen roads they missed these wild contests with the elements.

Sometimes trouble threatened when we were picnicking. A darkening sky, the distant rumble of thunder and the smell of rain on the dusty earth were signals for the frantic stowing of children and picnic gear and a quick departure. We usually managed to get home without much fuss, but one picnic was memorable, becoming known in the family annals as 'the day Mum drove home in the storm'. The main object of the outing was to gather firewood. After baiting up and setting a few fishing lines, we left Peter in charge and began to haul up wood to be stowed in the trailer. Neil then walked about a hundred yards further along a faint track to split up a large fallen gum branch. I began to cook the sausages while Anne and Beth set out the picnic plates. Then unbelievably the atmosphere became charged with pressure, the light took on a greenish tinge and the blue sky was obliterated by masses of rolling cloud. Peter salvaged the fishing gear and the twins packed up the picnic things while I rolled up the rug and picked up my pan of sausages. I wondered briefly what to do with them and then balanced the lot on the wood in the trailer. Everything was in the car ready to take off when I heard Neil bellowing in the distance. He was half way up the hill, beckoning with wild, extravagant gestures. With axe in hand he looked like an enraged axe-murderer as, through the rising sound of the storm, I heard him calling me to drive up towards him. I set off and when I approached he ran alongside the car and wrenched open the passenger-side door. 'Don't stop,' he shouted as I put my foot on the brake. 'Keep going. This is going to be a big one.'

Spurred on by his commands I roared up the hill, the trailer leaping and juddering as I desperately tried to avoid bumps and logs. I swung out onto the road with relief and drew up only to be met with another shouted admonition: 'Drive. Don't stop for anything.'

The rest of his message was drowned out as the first big drops whipped across the windscreen and a brilliant jag of lightning was followed by the crash of thunder. I put my foot down obediently, but in a few minutes the rain was pouring down and the road was a glistening stream. The car gave a sudden slide to the right and I panicked, 'You take over,' I yelled.

'Don't stop. We'll bog if you do. Just keep driving. The road's not sticky yet. You'll make it.'

The combined roarings of their father and the force of the storm had shocked the children into petrified silence and they sat clutching each other for support as we lurched through the pools of water. Then Christopher started up an anguished howl: 'Let Daddy drive. Let Daddy drive.' This did nothing for my morale as I peered through the streaming windscreen and muttered 'Steer into a skid' like a litany against disaster.

Then miraculously we were on the gravel stretch leading to the Mission entrance. I negotiated the grid and swept through the sea of water on the common. Then as I went through our gate, I braked. The ensuing skid took the car into a complete circle. It finished up with a miraculous slide into the open car shed where it stalled. There was complete silence for a moment then Beth, already a staunch defender of her sex, announced triumphantly, 'See. Mum is a good driver. Dad can't go into the shed like that.'

The girls were further convinced of my driving superiority when their father arrived home a few weeks later sopping wet and minus the car. The gubby truck was out of order and Len had asked Neil to take him into town for the weekly supplies. There had been several showers over the previous weeks but they took the chance that the hot sun would have dried out the road sufficiently. The trip in was completed successfully, but as they started home a sudden downpour made the road as slippery as glass. The car hit a rain-filled dip and slid sideways off the road where it settled in the mud. They trudged home through the rain and Len organised a team of young stalwarts to rescue the supplies. The same crew returned the next day to help Neil manoeuvre the car from the mire. They picked it up bodily and hauled it onto the road and then cheerfully supervised the drive home. They helped clear the mud from the car with the same noisy gusto they gave to any job that appealed to them. These boys worked prodigiously when invited to help, but moved at a snail's pace when coerced.

Like most people who live 'off the bitumen' we accumulated a store of tales about narrow escapes and minor adventures on the black soil roads, but our most hair-raising wet-weather experience was when we were returning from the long Christmas holidays in 1963. We visited friends and relatives and spent most of January camped near a grassy headland with the sea glittering before us and a green rainforest looming behind. Reluctant to leave, we postponed our return until the last week. On the way back we broke our journey at Tamworth staying with my sister Kath, her husband Tom, and their children. In spite of our former resolutions about arriving home with days to spare, we extended our stay till the last moment. Then on the Sunday we left early, thinking we'd be home late that afternoon. That would give Neil a whole day in school to prepare for the new year's work. It was less than he'd intended, but we were unworried as we drove west. Anne and Beth were agog with excitement as Tuesday was to be their first day at school, and we all cheerfully planned our activities for the next few days.

We left the bitumen and rattled along the gravel road to Langwell, noticing with some trepidation the sodden country and stretches of water on the road. In places we had to follow wheel tracks through detours around boggy patches, so that by the time we drove into Langwell we were considerably behind schedule. But we were unconcerned; we were on the home stretch with only about eighty miles to go. At the service station Neil asked about the condition of the road ahead and the attendant looked up from the petrol pump with a puzzled expression. 'You're not going to Yarrawina, are you, mate?' he asked. 'Where have you been lately? That road's been closed for days.'

He told us that a truck carrying perishable goods had tried to get through about three days earlier and having become bogged, had been rescued by tractors and towed to Yarrawina. The road had been left as a churned expanse of mud. He suggested that we book into a hotel for a day or two until the road dried and some repairs had been carried out. Devastated, we began a whispered conference on our plight. As usual we had eked out our money with just enough to get us home and though we had enough food and petrol we certainly couldn't run to the luxury of a hotel. Camping in the Langwell showground was not an attractive option and over-riding all was the knowledge that school started on Tuesday. There was no relief staff in those days and no excuses accepted for arriving late, especially after a school vacation. There were plenty of reasons for going on, but there were those miles of mud looming as a counterweight.

Two young men in a utility truck had listened to the advice proffered by the locals and noticed our earnest debate and evident indecision. They too had a deadline to meet further west and were anxious to get to Yarrawina that night and so offered to drive with us in convoy. That way there'd be two vehicles if towing were necessary and three men to push and dig if we struck trouble. We accepted their offer gratefully. Our two vehicles moved off to a chorus of dire prophecies from the locals and an ironic gibe from the attendant, 'See you in an hour or so, mate.'

With the utility following close behind we left the town and the firm gravelled road and soon reached the long expanse where two wheel tracks snaked through the mud. It got worse and there were frequent stops for discussion. Once saplings had to be cut and packed transversely over a stretch of swamp to form a corduroy. We rattled across it and then rebuilt it for the second vehicle. The sun was now setting, glinting rosily in the water holes on the road ahead. We usually avoided travelling after sunset because of the danger of hitting kangaroos and emus, but this fear at least was now remote. We were moving so slowly that even a tortoise would have been able to avoid a collision. Then we reached the place where the truck had bogged. It resembled a ploughed field. We unhooked the trailer and abandoned it on the side of the road with our bedding, our food and our camping gear.

Neil and one of the men had to walk beside the car, manhandling it bodily through the mud while I drove, trembling with fear and strain as I tried to keep to the wheel tracks. As we negotiated each bad patch they would return to help the utility through so that our progress was at a snail's pace. It grew dark and the weird noises of the bush began. But they were ignored, over-ridden by the revving of the two engines and the grunts and curses of the men as they slogged and shoved their way through the quagmire. When we were through the worst, Neil took over the driving and we crept forward over the higher ground towards Yarrawinna. The children had not spoken for an hour, not a whimper or protest as we battled through that nightmare stretch. They were cuddled together on the back seat and did not respond when I croaked out a reassurance that the worst was now over and we'd soon be home. Then, as we gathered speed, Peter remarked with masterly understatement, 'That was a bit of a strifle, wasn't it, Dad?' From that time on all our bad patches and experiences became 'strifles', chaotic situations where there was no alternative but to battle through.

The turn to the Mission loomed up and we stopped to say goodbye and offer fervent thanks to our two good Samaritans. They waved cheerfully and gathered speed towards Yarrawina. We turned slowly onto the Mission road, then came to an abrupt halt. A moving stream of water forty yards wide glinted in the headlights. The road had been cut completely. There was nothing to do but drive on to town. There we saw the utility truck parked in the main street and our two rescuers standing disconsolately beside it. They told us that the other roads out of town were also blocked and that Yarrawina had been isolated for days. So there were many stranded travellers and absolutely no accommodation. It was now about nine o'clock and we were exhausted and hungry, but by now I had become infected with the same stoic fatalism that the children displayed.

'See if you can buy some food and we'll sleep right here in the car,' I announced calmly. Neil nodded and walked up the dark street. The only lights came from the hotel; all the shops had closed hours before.

Several minutes later he returned, visibly relieved. His publican mate, Mick, had taken pity on us and offered to let us sleep in his upstairs residents' lounge if we did not mind makeshift bedding on the floor. Neil had even managed to fit in our two young saviours and it was a bedraggled, mud-caked group that trailed upstairs after our kindly host. As we washed away the murk, Mick's wife was busy heating up a huge tureen of soup and toasting rounds of bread. She helped me feed and bed down the children on the old-fashioned sofas and armchairs. Then I too crawled onto a mattress on the floor while Neil and the lads went down to the bar to be greeted with the hospitable reverence due to the first travellers to make it through from the outside.

Next morning Neil rang Len who said that the road in would

be impassable for some time and suggested we try the back way, the track that wound through the bush from town to a point on the river opposite the Mission. This was the short cut used by the Aborigines when the raft was operative. Unhappily it was also used by lecherous whites of all ages and status who drove out at night in search of what they termed 'a bit of black velvet'. Occasionally we heard them shouting their supposedly enticing invitations across the river, trying to attract the attention of those women they would not have spoken to in town.

Len also used this track. If there was sufficient warning that a flood was imminent, he would park the truck on the opposite bank and use the Mission boat to cross in emergencies. On this occasion he thought the water had gone down enough to make the crossing possible and told us to meet him at the river. We thanked Mick and his wife for the hospitality they had so freely dispensed and in half an hour were out at the clearing on the bank. It was a bright day and we could see the roof of our house glinting opposite. We were so close to home but found no consolation in that because the intervening sixty yards was a terrifying sight.

Our placid brown river was now a raging flood. The lower banks were feet under water and a slippery clay track led down to where Len waited in a tiny row boat, a nine-foot dinghy that looked too frail to survive in that torrent. It was tied to an exposed root and rocked and jerked alarmingly in the current. Two of the men stood on the track ready to help us into the boat and another group waited about a hundred yards down stream on the opposite side. We couldn't all cross at the one time and we had a terrible decision to make: the children had to be divided into two groups. It was obvious that as Neil was the stronger he should take three, just in case disaster struck. He slid down the bank and the men handed down Beth, Peter and Christopher. I stood clutching my two and watched the men untie the rope and push the boat off into the flood. The current was strong and Len had to row on a long diagonal course to get across. The small craft seemed to hesitate and then whirled away from the bank. A sad cry floated back to where I stood: 'Mummy, I don't like this boat.' I felt like Niobe, turned to a tear-stained rock with sorrow for my lost children as I watched them clinging grimly to their father. Incredibly Len was smiling as he rowed away with long, even strokes, despite appearing to make no progress against the current. Then unbelievably the boat began to inch its way to the opposite bank where Archie waited with outstretched arms. Len threw a rope, the boat was hauled ashore and willing hands lifted out the children. Neil and Len scrambled out and the boat was towed upstream to begin its journey back to us. It was not till then that I noticed the people lining the upper bank and saw how warmly they greeted and soothed the three children.

Now it was our turn. Anne, who had sobbed bitterly as she watched the others borne away on the flood, now nodded solemnly as I assured her there was nothing to worry about and that boat rides were fun. She was five and knew the importance of keeping up a pretence of cheerfulness in front of the younger ones. Soon Len was waiting below. Megan clung round my neck like a monkey and refused to let go so we had to be handed down together. Len steadied and seated us before lifting Anne back to me. Then we were off. It was not nearly as frightening in the boat as it had been watching the others and I managed to smile at Len's jokes about training for the Olympic Games. He had grown up messing about in boats on a large coastal river and was a good rower, but now he was battling the river for the fourth time. He certainly deserved our gratitude and I was glad that the voices cheering him from the bank were genuinely admiring.

Willing hands helped us up the clay bank and as we stood greeting everyone, reaction set in. I was relieved to be home but I felt so exhausted that I wanted only to collapse into a chair and be alone for a while. We moved up the path towards the house and as we topped the rise another surprise was in store. The once bare yard was now a jungle. Triffid-like weeds waved above our heads on either side of the path and the whole reserve was a lush green instead of the familiar brown. The hot, wet summer had transformed the place. We pushed open the door and the smell of mould was thick and rank. Worst of all, someone had closed the refrigerator door that I had so carefully propped open when I emptied it and turned it off six weeks before. Some helpful small person had undoubtedly noticed the open door and conscientiously shut it. The resultant smell called for immediate action so I gathered up soap powder and bleach and heated up the big black kettle. The holiday was over. Lying in bed that night with the worst of the mould routed, the weeds slashed from around the paths and the muddy clothes soaking in the wash tubs, I thought of the nightmare journey and the exhausting struggle to clean the old house. I remembered the visits we had made to friends living in neat, modern houses in trim, tidy towns. *Whatever are we doing out here?* I thought dismally. Just then a lugubrious voice came from the darkness beside me: 'You know, Pat, we must be mad.'

It was a week before Neil was able to get the car from where it stood over the river and to collect the trailer from the roadside where we had abandoned it. It says much for the honesty of the western people that nothing had been disturbed. The camping and fishing gear, the boxes of food and the bedding were all intact under the tarpaulin cover. The roads were now passable but water still lay in the hollows. In the centre of the Mission common a large, smelly lake of mud gleamed in the sun. One day I sent Peter on a message to school and on the way back he stood contemplating that smooth, inviting surface. Neil watched as Peter stepped back to get a good run up and then launched himself like a skier, his body crouched and his arms out for balance. Naturally he fell and as he scrambled up he quickly examined the damage to his clothes. Evidently thinking he might as well be hung for a sheep as the proverbial lamb, he took off again. He created spectacular patterns in the mud as he skated across, falling first on his back and then on his front, until he looked like a chocolate-coated gingerbread man. Neil sent one of the older boys to retrieve him and I heard Mrs Green laughing as she called me: 'Hey, Mrs Keating, I think Bunna's got a present for you'.

I looked up to see Bunna striding along, holding Peter at arms-length by the back of his shorts.

'Will I put him in the wash tub?' he asked, his usually solemn face split with a wide grin.

As I soaped and washed his sturdy, brown body, Peter gave me an angelic smile. 'Aren't you glad we're home, Mum?' he asked.

- 12 -

The Wrong Side of the Law

The mud and the mould that lingered after the January rains were nothing to the catastrophic situation at the school. During the third term of 1962 Neil had been devastated by the loss of his assistant, the talented and dedicated Merrita. The tiny settlement of Bingle, north-west of Yarrawina was left teacherless when the the young man appointed there walked off, rebelling no doubt against the isolation and the hardship he had endured for a year. A male teacher from the central school at Yarrawina was transferred to Bingle and Merrita was appointed to fill the vacancy in town. This was done with ruthless disregard for the wishes of the individuals concerned. There was no consultation and Neil heard of the move when Merrita arrived with the telegram ordering her to begin duty in town.

When it became obvious that no one was being transferred to fill the position at the Mission school, Neil complained bitterly. He stressed the impossibility of managing forty-eight pupils on his own, especially these children who needed so much individual attention. He pointed to the improvement in standards resulting from the schemes he and Merrita had initiated and worked so hard to implement. The inspector agreed that he was delighted with the progress that had been made and that it was impossible to expect this to continue with only one teacher. He hedged and prevaricated, promising to investigate ways of recifying this obvious injustice. The Area

Officer made soothing noises and vague promises, but no one arrived to fill the position.

Neil continued his barrage of phone calls and letters until a telegram arrived offering him a transfer to a larger school in a more favourable area. We were amazed at this as the 'two year tenure' was a rigid article of faith in those days and here he was being offered a move at the end of the first year. It seemed that the Department found it easier to rid themselves of this troublesome teacher than to correct the situation about which he complained. Then came another message: the proffered transfer had fallen through but if he soldiered on alone for the rest of the year he would be given an assistant at the beginning of 1963. So it was a bitter blow to arrive back after battling flood waters and near impassable roads to find that not only was there no assistant waiting, but none would be appointed at all.

The enrolment was well above the number approved for a two-teacher school. We discussed the possibility that the rough treatment was the result of treading on too many toes in the Welfare Department, but dismissed this as far-fetched. Surely Government Departments were not influenced by outside bodies to such an extent. Or was it that this community was so insignificant that it did not merit the same consideration as other places? We were sure of one thing only. This refusal to appoint a teacher for the twenty-odd infant children would not have occurred if they had been white. Neil was tempted to follow the example of the young Bingle teacher, but five children are a drawback when making such flamboyant gestures. So he began 1963 with a jaundiced view of his superiors. He continued to protest and his abrupt transfer in June of that year was most likely welcomed as much by the Regional Director as by the officers of the Welfare Board.

The parents and children were desolate when Merrita left. She was respected and loved and they were proud that someone of her calibre wanted to work with them. An Aboriginal woman recently told me that the Yarrawina children believed Merrita 'had Koori blood' somewhere in her ancestry. They thought she was too sympathetic, loving and understanding to be all white. I too was horrified when she departed. Not only did I sympathise with Neil's anger and the school's loss but I was sorry that Anne and Beth would now miss out on having her as a teacher. She was independent and determined in a time when these traits were not considered desirable womanly attributes. She wore her hair in a long black plait when fluffy curls were fashionable and reminded me of Jane Austen's independent, upright and delightful heroines. Like them she spiced her rectitude with a sharp sense of humour.

Neil had no option but to continue on alone with his unwieldy group of students and he soon became immersed in his work. Anne and Beth trotted off eagerly each day in their smart school clothes, delighted with their new role of grown-up school children. The three younger ones settled down quickly into their old carefree routine. I was busy with the usual chores and helped Neil out by preparing stencils and handwork for his lower classes. The holidays became as remote as a dream and our attention centred once more on the small world of the Mission.

Our complaints to the Welfare Board about the shakiness of the walls and the holes that gaped in the guttering and the verandah floor bore belated fruit. Two men from the Public Works Department arrived. They jumped up and down in the kitchen to show me how the walls had become detached from the ceiling joists. They crawled into the ceiling and under the house, emerging with lugubrious expressions to tell me that nothing could be done. 'She's got to be condemned, Missus,' said one, shaking his head solemnly. 'No good trying to fix it up. The whole set-up is going to close down in a year or two so it would be a waste of time and money doing any repairs.'

They went off to report formally to Neil, and I looked around at the ramshackle house, with its pleasing proportions and reclusive air, perched alone on the little knoll above the river. It had many faults but I prayed that it would outlast our stay. I had no desire to exchange it for a neat house in town. One thing the men had noted was that some of the doors and windows could not be shut, let alone locked and were a bit surprised when I mentioned that we were not particularly worried about that. Perhaps the only consolation of being poor is that the chances of burglary are remote. And we had never feared molestation of any sort. Country Australians rarely locked their doors in those days and our neighbours here had never given us any reason to act differently.

We had not been surprised or upset to find that someone had been inside the house and shut the fridge door during the long Christmas holidays. I suspected that some of the children occasionally wandered in while we were away. They did no harm and were most likely motivated by the same urge that causes people to join excursions through stately mansions — a desire to see how the other half lives. Even though by white standards our possessions were paltry, to these youngsters the house was full of exotic and interesting objects. The only trace of their passing was that occasionally a book would be closed, a cup washed or the teapot emptied. Only once had anything been taken; a jar of peanuts I had left on the table was opened and half the nuts eaten. I was only sorry they had not taken the lot and marvelled at the restraint shown by children faced with this temptation.

One or two things were taken from the school during these same holidays and that was the catalyst for one of the most shocking episodes of our stay. The articles were not much more valuable than our peanuts: an old school bell and some leather thonging from the handwork store and Neil was not unduly concerned about either. He suspected that they had disappeared during the New Year revels, not as a premeditated act of vandalism, but rather as an attempt to add noisy merriment to a party. But he had to report the forced and damaged door to get it repaired. He informed the local police and the Education Department in the prescribed manner and listed the items stolen. The Department approved the expenditure to fix the door and that should have been the end of the matter. Unless the damage was considerable, the police usually took only a cursory glance at these reports, even in those days when vandalism was uncommon. They knew that the time wasted on these matters rarely produced results and the reports were mostly acknowledged, filed and forgotten.

So Neil was surprised at the interest shown by one of the local sergeants in this trivial bit of petty crime. He not only questioned Neil carefully by phone but said he would be out personally to get a written statement. That seemed overly officious as he already had the necessary report and we wondered why a school bell merited the attention of the second-in-command, the redoubtable Sergeant Brownridge. We concluded that all must have been quiet on the crime front in Yarrawina.

The next evening the police car rolled up to our door with the Segeant and a young constable aboard. The Sergeant stepped out first and stood for a moment surveying the Mission. He was a bulky man with a dark, jowled face and massive shoulders and arms. He swaggered up the path followed by his assistant. He greeted Neil, who had met him once in town, with jocose familiarity and beamed at me as we were introduced.

'No, we won't come inside,' he murmured genially in answer to Neil's invitation. 'Musn't interrupt the little woman in her evening chores. This table on the verandah will do nicely.'

He seated himself at the table and Neil drew up two chairs for himself and the constable. Recognising that I had been dismissed, I withdrew to the kitchen, ostensibly to perform the duties of a good 'little woman'. I stationed myself against the wall by the window where I could see a little and hear everything. The sergeant lounged back comfortably, chatting cheerfully about our holidays on the coast, the weather and such items while his eyes roved across the deserted reserve. I could sense the silent watchers hiding in their houses, noting every move made by this feared and powerful man. He too was aware of their scrutiny; all his gestures seemed to challenge them to note his presence and wonder why he was there.

Then he straightened up and got down to the purpose of his visit, the burglary, as he termed it. He said that he knew the culprits, two boys from the Mission and their friend from the river settlement. He alleged that these lads were responsible for several similar break-ins in town and he had been trying to nail them for some time. Now he had them. Neil asked how he knew their identity and the sergeant smiled knowingly. 'We have ways of finding out these things. They've been tentatively identified several times. Now I've got them for sure. Stealing on their own home turf. Couldn't have been anyone but them.'

Neil began a question about the reasons for connecting a school break-in with those in town, but the sergeant interrupted again.

'It's no big deal. A few months in gaol will do them the world of good. It'll teach them a lesson and set them on the right path.'

My instant reaction was disbelief. A few months' gaol — for the theft of a school bell? The sergeant must have read the same message on Neil's face, as he immediately became formal and official. He pulled out three typewritten sheets from a large envelope and, turning to the last page, put his finger on a dotted line.

'We've prepared a statement,' he said producing a fountain pen. 'If you will sign here we need trouble you no longer.'

Neil put down the pen and shook his head. 'I can't sign till I've read it,' he objected.

The sergeant sat motionless for a moment and then passed over the papers with a muttered remark about wasting time. Neil began to read but stopped half-way down the page.

'What's this rubbish? You've got here that I reported a burglary last September. Our house has never been burgled. Where did you get all this about the theft of household goods? This is a pack of lies.'

The sergeant stood up and reached for the papers, an angry red mottling his face. But Neil waved him away and turned the page. He skimmed quickly and gave another outraged snort.

'Good God, man. This is not what was stolen from the school. I reported the loss of a bell and some leather. And we've never noticed these boys hanging around. We don't even know them.'

The sergeant leaned forward and murmured confidentially, 'Listen, mate, there may be a few exaggerations here and there, but you'll be doing me a big favour if you sign it. These boys are troublemakers. We'd really appreciate it if you'd help us put them behind bars for a spell.'

'No fear,' Neil answered. 'This is just a frame-up. I'm not signing that.'

The sergeant snatched the papers. His face was dark with anger and his voice icy, 'You're causing us a lot of trouble over a few typing errors. But if you insist, I'll come back with another statement tomorrow.' He strode down the steps but then turned. 'We won't forget how well you co-operated,' he said sarcastically and marched off to the car. The constable rose, his embarrassed blush sweeping up to meet his ginger hair. He uttered his second comment for the evening. 'Good evening,' he muttered and stood irresolute for a second. His mouth opened twice and then he scurried down to the waiting car and off they sped.

We were amazed at the blatancy of the frame-up and the Sergeant's assumption that we would be ready to connive at such a crude injustice. We had known of police in country towns who received rake-offs from the publican, the S.P. bookie and anyone else who wished to indulge in shady pursuits. That was regarded as a fairly normal part of a policeman's lot, but we had never been involved. Along with the majority of the population we regarded the term 'crooked cop' as an amusing bit of tautology, but our knowledge of their machinations came to us from newspapers or local gossip. Now we were directly involved with an attempt to pervert the course of justice. We discussed the matter earnestly and were rather proud that Sergeant Brownridge's attempt to convict the boys would fail because of Neil's firm stand. What innocents we were to think that a man like that would accept defeat easily.

The next day was Saturday and after working in the school all the morning Neil wandered down to the river for a few hour's fishing. About four o'clock I saw the police car drive up to the manager's house and park by the office gate. The same men got out and walked inside. I knew that Neil would be home soon to avoid the onslaught of mosquitoes at sundown and I waited impatiently for him, not wanting to be alone with the sergeant and his awkward off-sider. Time dragged past and I wondered why they were taking so long reporting to Len. Just as I had decided that their visit had no connection with us, a teenage lad came through the office gate and ran towards our house.

'Mrs Keating,' he called from our steps. 'The policeman wants Mr Keating to come to the Big House straight away.'

'Oh, does he?' I answered indignantly. 'If that policeman wants Mr Keating he should have the manners to come over here and see him. Go back and tell him that.'

'But he's got to come,' the poor frightened boy whispered imploringly. 'The Boss said I had to come and get him. The police want him.'

'He does not have to obey their orders. Tell them to come over here,' I replied curtly.

The boy dropped his head and stood in an agony of indecision. I repented immediately. He looked so miserable standing there in his tattered shorts and singlet and I knew that it was impossible for such a boy to relay a defiant message to those powerful men. 'No, I don't mean that. Tell the sergeant Mr Keating has gone fishing, so you were not able to give him the message. Then say that, if he would like to call over here in half an hour, Mr Keating will see him.'

The boy looked up. His vaguely familiar features were now impassive and he nodded and turned away.

'What are you doing over there?' I asked. 'Did the policeman want to see you? Is he questioning you about something?'

He shrugged and gave me a bewildered glance. 'Don't you know?' he asked softly and walked off down the path.

Neil strolled back from the river about ten minutes later and as he approached the house the sergeant left the office and walked across to meet him at the gate. The sergeant handed over an envelope and Neil extracted the single sheet of paper. He read it and nodded, 'Yes. I'll sign this,' he said.

They walked up to the same table on the verandah and the policeman handed him a pen and waited while Neil glanced over the sheet again. It was a simple statement that the school had been entered illegally and a bell and some leather thonging were now missing. The date when it had been reported was correct and the whole statement took up three lines. He nodded and picked up the pen. The sergeant's index finger pointed to where the word 'Signature' followed by a row of dots appeared in the bottom right-hand corner of the page. Neil signed on the dotted line and with a brief exchange of farewells Sergeant Brownridge departed.

Years later Neil discovered how easily he had been duped. He was recounting the episode to a friend when he was interrupted at this point by an incredulous laugh. George was an old ambulance officer and there was little he had missed in years of observing human behaviour.

'You were green, Keato, a real babe in the woods,' George laughed. 'That's one of the oldest tricks in the police book. You sign at the bottom of the page and they go back to the station and type in what they like in the empty space above.'

Back then, we suspected nothing and thought that the whole affair was over. The Department replaced the broken lock and the bell and we forgot the matter. Occasionally, I noticed a coolness in the attitude of some of the people from the Mission. It was an almost imperceptible lack of warmth and spontaneity, but even Mrs Green professed ignorance when I broached the subject, so I put it all down to my imagination. Then I heard that the three boys had been arrested and were in Dubbo awaiting trial. They had been charged with break and enter and stealing and I was thankful we had nothing to do with the charge. I told Mrs Green how the sergeant had tried to involve us in his frame-up and she was not at all astonished by my revelations.

'Well, I reckon if the police want to get you for something they will. There's no way you can beat them. They'll always win because it's your word against theirs. So those boys better grin and bear it.'

We continued to believe that we had no involvement in the case and the boys had been picked up for other misdemeanours, those 'break-ins in town' that the sergeant had mentioned. In our ignorance we thought that if the police had wanted to use Neil's statement as extra evidence then Neil would have been notified to appear in court. So I was dismayed when a woman appeared at my door one morning, looking tired and distressed. I had seen her often and knew her by name, but otherwise she was a stranger to me. She told me that she was the mother of one of the boys who had been arrested and that she had just returned from Dubbo. Their trial had taken place two days before and the boys had been sentenced to several months in gaol. Her voice broke and she began to cry.

'Mrs Keating, my boy didn't do that to you. He didn't break into your house. None of them did. They never stole them things from you. All that stuff that was pinched – it wasn't them that did it.'

I stood horrified as she sobbed out her protests. Then I realised what she was saying. Her son had been accused of burgling our house. The stolen goods listed were those mentioned in Brownridge's first statement and it was obvious he had somehow based his charge on that fabrication. I attempted to break in to her lament, but she continued on mournfully repeating her son's innocence until at last I shook her by the shoulders.

'Stop and listen,' I begged. 'This is all wrong. The police can't have charged them with stealing our things. Tell me exactly what was said in court.'

Then a calm voice of reason broke in and Myrtle Green pushed the distraught woman into a chair. 'We all better have a cup of tea,' she said. 'You tell your story first, Millie, and then we'll hear what Mrs Keating has to say.'

Millie began a confusing version of the evidence presented in court. The part relating to our supposed burglary was a short statement that the theft had been reported after our return from holidays in September and several items were listed as missing. It had been thought that the perpetrators of the act were from the Mission and this was confirmed by the break-in at the school. This is my understanding of what was said in court, garnered from Millie's rambling and repetitious account, interspersed as it was with meandering asides and anguished protests. My mind focused on one thing only. All else was irrelevant beside the fact that Sergeant Brownridge had apparently used that first statement which he had concocted, even though Neil had rejected it as untrue. The boys may have been guilty of breaking into buildings in town, they may have foolishly made off with the school bell, or they may have been innocent of both charges. I had no idea, but I did know that part of the evidence used against them was a lie, and that lie had been contrived by the police.

I told the women what had happened on the two occasions we had met Sergeant Brownridge and to my surprise they did not react with the horrified astonishment I had expected. They seemed to accept the inevitable injustice of the white man's law and that it was useless to protest against it. They were happy to know that we had not made up a lie to use against them but took it for granted that policemen would have no compunction about lying to gain their ends.

I leapt up. 'I'm going to do something about this,' I announced 'I'm going to ring the police station and lodge a protest.'

There was a chorus of dismayed objections, both women assuring me that it was not only a waste of time but it would do me no good to antagonise the police. Fired with indignation, I swept their protests aside and asked them to wait with the children until I returned. I marched across to the office, imbued with a righteous glow which began to abate as I dialled the number and waited to see who would answer. I was greatly relieved when I recognised the voice of the Crown Sergeant, the man in charge, who had the reputation of being the kindly, reasonable face of the law in Yarrawina. When I dramatically announced that I wanted to lodge a complaint against his second-in-command and told him why, he suggested soothingly that it would be better if I came in and discussed the matter with him personally. He would be able to see me at two o'clock that afternoon. I hesitantly asked if Sergeant Brownridge would be there and I was pleased to hear that he was still in Dubbo.

Confidently I returned to assure the women that I would most likely be able to have the verdict overturned and justice meted out to the boys and the policeman alike. Mrs Green promised to baby-sit while I went off to start my crusade; and Millie said she would return later to hear about it. We all parted with varying degrees of optimism. Neil's reaction when he came home for lunch was dampening. As I poured out the whole story his face darkened with anger and then slowly assumed an expression of long-suffering dismay. He agreed that it was a most flagrant flouting of justice and we should certainly protest, but he was very uneasy about letting me loose against the law. He suggested that I ring back and make another appointment for a time when he was free. I thought of my flamboyant posturing and promises and realised what a fool I would look.

'Well, I'm the one who has to tell Millie that it's been postponed and she will think that I'm like all the rest, all talk and no action. And Brownridge will be back in a day or two, so we should see the Crown Sergeant before they have time to talk it over. Anyway, why can't I report a crime as well as you?'

Neil gave up, agreeing that as the appointment had been made, I might as well go. I assured him that if we were summoned in later to face Sergeant Brownridge, he certainly could do all the talking. My task would be to set the wheels of justice turning while he orchestrated the main campaign. So, with warnings about keeping calm and rational ringing in my ears, I set off.

I rehearsed the story all the way to town and told it calmly and rationally to the Sergeant. I started with the missing bell and after describing in detail our two encounters with his subordinate, I finished with Millie's account of the charges laid against the boys. The officer listened politely to all I had to say. His face was impassive and when I stopped and stared expectantly, he sat for a minute or two in silence. Then he shook his head gravely.

'I understand your surprise and anger at what has happened,' he said earnestly. 'There certainly seems to have been some mix up and I'm afraid Sergeant Brownridge is at fault. But you must understand he is a diligent officer with a very difficult job and it is no wonder he makes an occasional mistake. This is what stress and overwork can do.'

'But this was no mistake,' I broke in. 'This was a deliberate attempt to falsify evidence. He had written that first statement before he even interviewed Neil. It was a complete fabrication and he admitted as much by drawing up the second one.'

'Was the second statement correct?'

'Yes, but it was the first one that was used in court. We can't understand why it was admitted as evidence if it wasn't signed.'

'Well, I will look into that, certainly. You are sure Neil did not sign it, are you?'

'Of course, I'm sure. Anyhow, why wasn't Neil called to court as a witness if he had reported a theft?'

'There was no need,' he smiled. 'The sergeant had his statement.'

The logic of that argument astounded me and I shut up for a minute. I felt I was getting nowhere. My objections met with a barrier of seemingly sympathetic words that channelled any debate away from the real crux of the matter.

'Well, something has to be done about these boys,' I retorted. 'If we sued Brownridge for falsifying evidence the case would be dismissed and they would be released. That seems the only thing to do.'

The Sergeant then told me at length about the huge expense involved in bringing a charge against anyone, especially a policeman who would have access to police lawyers. He wondered if we could really afford the time and money involved in what would be a major case. Accusations of perjury were serious and this case would not be a simple matter of appearing before a local magistrate. My confidence ebbed away. We had no knowledge of the law and no money. I listened with sore resignation as the Sergeant brought out his second argument. There was no reason to believe that a second case would ensure the boys' release. After all, our statement was not the only one, as other people had laid charges against the boys, and they had been pronounced guilty in those instances.

'You're not suggesting that all that evidence was falsified as well, are you?' he asked.

I shook my head dumbly and stood up. 'There's no point in going on with this, is there?' I faltered, close to angry tears. 'You're not going to do anything about it and that terrible man is going to get off scott free.'

'I promise I will look into the matter. I will do what I can for the boys. They are first offenders and should be due for remission after a time. I will interview Sergeant Brownridge when he returns, but I suggest you and your husband try to forget the matter. It is up to you. If you wish to proceed, please come in and lay a formal charge. I will regard our meeting this afternoon as an informal chat, quite off the record.'

He ushered me to the door. 'I really do sympathise with the Aborigines, you know. I have tried to help them but every situation seems weighted against them. There is only so much one man can do.'

I had to admit that they all spoke well of him, but their attitude towards the police was shaped more by the fear inspired by his deputy than any effort he made. Then I asked why Yarrawina had five policemen when there were only a thousand people in the whole shire. He conceded that the disproportionately large staff was solely because of Yarrawina's numerous Aborigines. The police were certainly not needed to protect the whites from black violence. That was a fairly rare occurrence and black versus black attacks were in about the same proportion as assault in the white community, so why the need for so many police?

I mentioned that the most noticeable police activity was the rounding up of Aboriginal drinkers. The paddy waggon was a familiar sight, especially at weekends, as it cruised the streets gathering up men from the parks and the lanes behind the hotels. If that was the reason for the large police presence it was surely a waste of money and man power.

'I don't make the laws,' he answered, 'and I will be glad when that particular law is overturned.' Then he looked sharply at me. 'And I don't give the blacks a bad time in the cells either. I see that they get a good night's sleep and have a decent breakfast before they go home.'

He was evidently a mind-reader as well as being a plausible, friendly fellow. He opened the car door for me and then shook hands, 'Try not to get too upset about the things you see and hear out here,' he said. 'God knows things could not be too much worse for most of the Aborigines but, although you might not believe it, the situation has improved over the years. I think it will continue to do so and I hope there will be some changes soon.'

He was right in a way. Things improved in Yarrawina when Sergeant Brownridge was transferred a month later at about the same time as the repeal of the law banning Aboriginal drinking. Only the police and the black population know whether the Crown Sergeant was right when he spoke of the continuing improvements in relations between the two groups. Now more than thirty years on we read of black deaths in custody and dawn raids at Redfern and wonder how much has been gained.

Neil was waiting with the two women in the kitchen and as I told my tale I realised what a futile exercise it had all been. My attempt to right a wrong had been no more than a nuisance and a waste of time. Nothing would be done. In most people's eyes the case was insignificant and police solidarity would ensure that there would be no mention of false statements or perjury. Not for a moment have we believed that the later transfer of the Sergeant had anything to do with his behaviour on that occasion. So the unimportant little saga was soon forgotten, except by Millie and the boys who all had to accept that their experience of our judicial system was tainted by corruption and that they were powerless to redress it.

I wrote to her son while he was in gaol, but received no answer. Neither did we find out how long he served as it was less than six months before we too left the area.

The repeal of the law forbidding the consumption of alcohol by Aborigines put an end to one of the most visible symbols of discrimination, the regular police round up of black drinkers. These men must have resented the ignominy of being hustled into paddy waggons while their white counterparts drank with impunity nearby, but I learnt later that they had even more reason for their hatred of the practice. One of the Aborigines from Yarrawina told me that some of the police were not above transferring cash from the prisoners' pockets into their own as they searched them before they were placed in the cells. This financial transaction could range from the usual few shillings to several pounds if a shearer had just cashed his cheque. Of course the Aborigines knew there was no point in protesting as it was their word against that of a police officer.

This exploitation gave rise to an episode that caused our friend Ray to become a folk hero as well as laying the foundation for the bitter enmity that grew between him and the dreaded Sergeant. Ray had arrived back in town after weeks away in the shearing sheds. His pockets were full of cash and he treated his friends on the river bank to a convivial afternoon of drinking and yarning before he decided to head home to the Mission. As they strolled up to the taxi rank in the main street the paddy waggon drew up and the sergeant and a constable alighted.

They shoved the nearest couple of men into the back of the waggon and then turned to Ray. The sergeant caught him by the arm and attempted to push him into the van. Ray resisted and they struggled together until Ray managed to throw his adversary on his back in the gutter. Kneeling upon his chest he began to haul on the policeman's tie, tightening it till the sergeant's face turned blue. Fortunately, the constable, helped by frightened on-lookers, was able to drag Ray to his feet. A murder trial was averted but a legend was started. Ray had taken on the enemy and beaten him, earning the admiration always accorded the underdog who bites back, be he Ned Kelly, Robin Hood or an Aborigine protecting his liberty and his pay.

Laws were not enforced as rigorously for the white section of the community. Neil's first meeting with Sergeant Brownridge occurred early in 1962 during a so-called raid on illegal drinkers one Sunday morning. The law permitted bona-fide travellers to be served and Neil qualified, having travelled the required ten miles to the hotel, but he rose uneasily when whispered warnings of a raid flew round the crowded bar. He was ready to join the drinkers who were already fleeing through the back doors when a heavy hand caught his arm.

'Sit down, son. I think it's your shout.' The sergeant smiled jovially and turned to the barman. 'Two more please, Mick.'

The group of local businessmen who were sitting with him grinned at Neil and resumed their conversations, seemingly oblivious to the fact that two uniformed policemen were moving through the bar questioning individual drinkers. The raid flowed past them and the group finished their drinks with impunity. Neil had experienced the privilege of being on the right side of the law. A year later that comforting feeling was gone and we were very relieved to read in the local paper a notice informing everyone of the sergeant's transfer. Our feelings were shared by most blacks in the community and I'm sure Ray celebrated enthusiastically.

- 13 -
Worlds Apart

Our encounters with floods and police were an exciting start to the new year, but life soon settled into its usual routine and our interests became focused once more on our small, isolated community. News of the outside world barely filtered through the barrier of concerns about the children, the school and the people around us. News items about the Kennedys, gossip about Marilyn Monroe and tales of Royalty paled into insignificance when we could speculate on Eva and Essie and their swains. The oratory of the politicians was never as gripping as a speech made by Mary when she publicly denounced the Matron and all her works, nor could their proclamations have brought such swift and devastating action.

We were aware that many people on the outside regarded our situation with a mixture of horror and pity. When we spent the September holidays of 1962 with my mother and step-father on their small property in the western Darling Downs we got a similar reaction. My mother was relieved to find that the children were flourishing and happy, Ned was sceptical about the ability of any Aborigine to reach white educational standards and both were anxious that we should soon return to a more 'normal' situation. Their neighbours were inclined to believe that we were imbued with a desire to convert the heathen blacks, or else that Neil had failed in the usual school system and had descended to the lowest rung of his profession. Their anecdotes about Aborigines were all slanted to prove the innate superiority of the speakers and usually started with '. . . Not that I've anything against blacks, of course'.

The same thing happened during our Christmas holidays on the coast and we realised that while our involvement with the Aborigines bored and annoyed many people, our interest in the usual concerns of white society had lessened considerably. Just one year on the Mission had caused a drastic change in our lives. Previously we had known few Aborigines; now we mixed with few white people and had become somewhat alienated from their values. Apart from Val and Merrita we knew hardly anyone in Yarrawina and there was little incentive for us to visit the town, except for shopping. We considered the open-air picture theatre but rejected it, finding that the fare it offered was scarcely worth the worries of baby-sitters and the long trip in. Our swimming holes and fishing spots were more attractive than those in town and we found the friends we had made on the Mission were more appealing than the occasional acquaintances we had made outside.

My only foray into Yarrawina society was not a success. I had been invited to meet a group of young married women, the wives of teachers, bank officers and other officials of that stratum who had been thrown together because their husbands were doing their stint in this western town on their way up the promotion ladder. I was quite pleased at the prospect of an afternoon of freedom from the family, of gossip and laughter uninhibited by the presence of husbands and children, and drove up to the house in high spirits.

The hostess was the wife of the local headmaster, a tall, elegant blonde named Eloise, who greeted me with hospitable warmth. Her friends were equally welcoming and we settled down to chat over a rather sweet light wine. I found out whose husband went with which job and caught the subtle intimation of a pecking order based on the rank attained by those same husbands. The wives of the assistant station-master and the bank teller had to try a little harder than did those of the men who had attained top ranking. In that case, I thought, I should be making a great effort, but it seemed that my status as a newcomer to the group assured me attention.

As Eloise refilled the glasses we progressed to children. My admission that I had five under school age brought squeals of delighted shock and murmurs of well-bred sympathy. Used to this reaction, I defensively proceeded to relate a few incidents to subtly prove the charm and intelligence of my off-spring and my ability to overcome difficulties. This led to a mention of conditions on the Mission, the lack of electricity and other amenities and the earlier difficulties we had experienced. The company was galvanised into action. They had studiously avoided the subject, but now having been given an opening, their questions poured forth.

I managed to convey that we were quite happy with our new home, that we found the people there to be kind, generous and interesting and that, most importantly, I found it a great place in which to bring up children. This caused a lull until Eloise asked if I was going to bring the twins in to school by car each day or did we intend to take up residence in town by the start of the new year. My disclaimer was not well received and it was implied that we were sacrificing our children for some vague principle. As this was only about a month after Christopher's experience of segregation and I was still guiltily worried that he might have suffered psychological harm, my facade of well-bred detachment cracked. I went on about the conditions under which the Aborigines lived, the historical background for their degradation and the necessity for a radical change in white attitudes. While some of the ladies agreed, a few sharply repudiated my charges and it seemed that the tea party had foundered. Then a rather insipid little woman leaned forward eagerly, her eyes gleaming with excitement.

'But aren't you frightened out there alone all day when Neil's at school?' she murmured. 'I'm terrified even here in the white part of town. Harry always insists that I keep the house locked all the time he's at work, even in the daytime.'

'Frightened? No, certainly not,' I answered. 'What is there to be scared of out there?'

'Well, you know, the men . . . ,' she whispered in her agitation.

'You know what they say about black men, how they are always wanting to have a white woman. Aren't you scared?'

'Good God. What utter rot,' I interrupted rudely. 'All the black men I know prefer their own black women. Which is more than I can say for a lot of the white men from the town here. They are the greatest menace to womankind I have ever seen, driving out in the night to try and snaffle some poor young black girls.'

Gathering up my belongings as I spoke, I turned to Eloise. 'I really must go,' I said. 'It's getting late and the children will be waiting for me. Thank you very much. It has been delightful.'

She accompanied me out to the car. 'I understand, Pat,' she said. 'I find many things upsetting too. You must come again and do ring me if you need any help.'

I smiled and nodded, thinking it was unfair to label all tall, elegant blondes as patronising and that she most likely was sincere. Then she bent towards the car window.

'Do give my love to Neil. I knew him at college and we all used to think he'd go far in the Department. Ah well, there are other things in life, aren't there?'

After I drove around the corner, my friendly wave turned into a rude gesture and even though I seethed with rage, I could not help grinning at the thought of the avid discussions now taking place over the remains of the cucumber sandwiches and dainty cakes.

In many ways Yarrawina seemed to have two faces. At first we thought it a totally cold and heartless town with the Aborigines pushed to the outskirts, harassed by authority and despised by most of the white inhabitants. But we were to learn of the ones who were without prejudice, those who mixed as comfortably with the black half of the community as they did with their colleagues, whether from the hospital, the school, the shops or the local stations. We often speculated whether those who were born and brought up in the area were more or less bigotted than those who came in from outside. Only the Aborigines themselves could decide that.

Two brothers ran the big department store that had been owned by their family for many years and they seemed to treat everyone with impartiality. One of them told Neil that the

Aborigines kept the town solvent. They always paid cash, whereas the townspeople mainly settled their accounts once a month and the squatters paid up maybe once a year, providing their wool cheque came in as expected. These two men were unfailingly courteous with all their customers, squatter or shearer, black or white and we placed them on the merit side of the ledger. The man and wife who presided over the town cafe were also pleasant and helpful to all, providing a meeting place for the youth of both colours, as well as dispensing ice-creams and lollies and managing to make delicious milk-shakes with powdered milk. The newsagent was a notable character. He was witty and intelligent and we were often amused by his comments on politics and social trends. He sometimes pointed out an article and invited our opinion, following it up by a biting critique of the writer or the subject matter. He was very relieved when we cancelled the *Bulletin* after its sale to the Packer newspaper syndicate and with the same disregard for profits, he once berated me for ordering a well-known women's magazine, relenting only when I explained my reasons for buying it. He enjoyed his role of acerbic old iconoclast, but we discovered another side to him.

As cracker night approached the newsagency became a treasure trove of gaudy fireworks and Neil decided to buy pretty sparklers to amuse our children and their friends. The newsagent remarked that he didn't sell crackers to the town kids. When Neil asked why, he told him that he kept them for a display on the night itself. In that way all the children could enjoy the show, not just the few who could afford them. Some of the other business men joined in with free lollies and drinks and the night had grown into a town institution. No longer did the little have-nots from the river bank have to watch enviously from afar as their wealthier counterparts enjoyed the usual private parties. He displayed the fireworks for weeks beforehand because he believed that the anticipation was more enjoyable than the actual treat. These instances of genuine sympathy leavened, but could not dissipate, the general atmosphere of intolerance that pervaded the town. It seemed to be accepted by most that the blacks were of lesser importance than the whites.

The social life of the town may have been scintillating, but our five children, the miles of gravel road and our small bank balance were all reasons for remaining out on the Mission, so it was just as well we found plenty to interest us there. Life was certainly not an unruffled pastoral idyll though and on many occasions we regretted leaving the convenience of civilisation. When I developed an abscessed tooth it meant a trip over seventy miles of corrugated road to a town with a resident dentist. The memory of that trip with a throbbing jaw, a grizzling baby and a car-sick Anne vomiting over her siblings remains in my mind as a reason for staying safely on the coast. Most of our complaints were minor. We grumbled about the lack of music other than the country-and-western songs favoured by the local radio station, we fought for possession of each new cross-word puzzle, reread every book and soon learnt that early to bed was not only a prelude to wisdom, health and riches but an absolute necessity in the back-blocks. Life however had a pleasant, bucolic simplicity and we gained much satisfaction from gathering loads of wood, catching a feed of fish and growing our own vegetables.

The darker side of the picture was the constant battle against flies, mosquitoes, ringworm and lice. I was shocked at my first sight of a louse scurrying through Megan's fine baby hair, and all the more when I examined the other four heads. A strenuous campaign waged with expensive lotions from the chemist would give a short respite but inevitably we would all be scratching again in a few weeks. I rejected Shirley's advice about segregating the children from their friends and tried all sorts of remedies, even resorting to shampooing with kerosene, a drastic measure that left us with sore scalps and shiney but smelly hair. Then Neil started a grand scheme for delousing the whole village. He got a bulk supply of lotion from the hospital and handed it out at school to all comers. Combined with rigorous vigilance this worked quite well and that particular plague, though never conquered altogether, became manageable.

Then came ringworm and it took me some time to discover the source and why Christopher was the main victim. He and Peter slept on the verandah and it became the favoured refuge of the stray cats of the village. They seemed to ignore Peter except for one scrawny female he surreptitiously encouraged. She subsequently rewarded him by having kittens in his bed one morning at dawn. The rest preferred Christopher and curled up happily round his soft, chubby body. I swathed the beds with mosquito nets and crept out at night to shoo the cats, but to no avail. One battered specimen always slept on his pillow and I came to suspect she was the ringworm carrier. We used pots of ointment and shaved his hair to a faint, golden stubble but his scalp was constantly infected. I mentioned my suspicions to Mrs Green and she told me not to worry; she would solve the problem. Sure enough that afternoon we heard a commotion on the outskirts of the village. There was a lot of yelling and even the sound of shooting in the scrub behind the houses and when we investigated we were proudly informed that the men had killed all the mangey cats. That put an end to the ringworm problem and any guilt I felt about the cat slaughter faded when I realised that we could let Christopher's hair grow again.

In September we joined half of the State in suffering the so-called Asian flu and by the time I had nursed the other six through it I was a real cot-case. I dragged around for weeks full of self-pity which only evaporated when I saw how the rest of the Mission had been affected. One of the old men had died and several people had been taken to hospital. I wondered how anyone survived such a disease in those cramped and draughty houses where the lack of privacy and comfort was as much a bar to recovery as the lack of antibiotics.

All through the summer we battled 'fly-eye' as everyone called it. It was a fly-borne malady that caused the eyelids to swell enormously while the eye became very sore and itchy. I soon learnt to catch it early at the first sign of swelling and apply drops and ointment, so my children were lucky. They did not have to wait the extra hours till the clinic opened and the remedies were handed out. We often saw children whose eyes were mere red slits between swollen, purple lids, stoically silent as a runny discharge trickled down their cheeks. No amount of care could have kept the flies from their faces but the possession of such simple things as eye-drops, cotton wool and even clean water would have prevented a lot of pain.

As I battled against these infections I often thought of the comments I'd heard about 'dirty' Aborigines, usually made as the speaker noticed the symptoms of these same diseases — runny eyes and noses, sores and scabs. It was as though the Aborigines had a monopoly on these anti-social things. I remembered that some of the families in the little mining town I had lived in during the depression were shunned as being dirty, lousy and infective and they were white. It was poverty not colour that was the culprit. Insect screens cost money as do ointments and medicines. The Aborigines suffered the opprobrium of these illnesses as well as the pain and discomfort.

The biggest worry was what we called summer diarrhoea. My children were well-fed and healthy and I had access to medicines, so for me it was just another nuisance — more washing to do, fretful children to soothe, and a few disturbed nights. The other mothers must have dreaded the hot weather with the increase in fly-borne diseases. I heard of the deaths that occured in the western reserves without understanding that they may have been caused by those illnesses that we classed as minor. Then in our second summer several children on the Mission became quite ill and one died in shocking circumstances.

It was late one Saturday afternoon when Shirley arrived with a message. Neil had gone fishing with Laurie, the children were playing peacefully and I invited her to sit and talk for a while. As we sat looking over the Mission, one of the young women came towards us carrying her baby. She looked quite upset as she turned in our gate and walked hesitantly up the path.

'Will you have another look at the baby, Matron?' she asked. 'She's worse than she was this morning. I'll have to take her into hospital.'

The girl pulled back the shawl and I gasped with surprise. The baby was about three months old and I remembered how lively and pretty she had looked when I'd last seen her. Now she lay still and limp, her eyes glazed and dull.

Shirley spoke coldly. 'I told you how to treat her. And there's no way you're going to town to-day, Cathie. I know what you want to do. You want to go to that big party on the river bank. I wasn't born yesterday so don't try those tricks on me. Take her home; feed her. If you're still worried tomorrow, come back and see me in the morning.'

'But she's really sick,' the girl protested, 'She won't feed at all. She just lies there — she doesn't even cry.'

'That's a really bad sign,' I interjected. 'I think it might be a good idea to see the doctor, Shirley.'

'Oh do you really think so,' she retorted angrily. 'Well, I am the Matron here and I'll decide who's to see the doctor and when. I'll thank you to keep out of this. Len has been working all day on the wretched pump and I'm not asking him to drive into town to-night. It's the Sabbath and he hasn't had any rest at all!'

She strode down the path, ushering the girl towards the gate. I could hear her wrathful tones as the two moved off across the common and knew that I had made things worse by interfering. Shirley would now be more determined than ever. It wasn't my business and I'd better forget about it, I thought, as I went inside to bath and feed the children. But I kept seeing that lifeless little face and I resolved to interfere even further. I searched in the medicine cupboard and found a packet of glucose mixture the chemist had given me when Megan had been sick. He'd assured me that it was absolutely harmless and that, mixed with boiled water would help prevent dehydration. I sterilised one of the bottles and a teat that Megan had long abandoned and made up the correct dose. By now it was dark and the children were dressed in their pyjamas. I asked them if they knew where Cathy with the little baby lived. Of course they did and danced with delight when I suggested a walk. Stressing the importance of being quiet and sedate when out walking at night, we started off through the deserted streets. I felt both guilty and defiant and was greatly relieved when we were out of sight of the Big House.

Cathie's mother opened the door when I called from the gate. She stared in surprise to see me there surrounded by pyjama-clad children. She must have thought I was making an ill-timed social call so I hurriedly explained that I was worried about the baby. Cathy appeared in the doorway beside her. She looked no more than a child herself standing in the pale lamp light and I banished any guilty doubts that still lingered.

'Cathie, here's some mixture from the chemist. If the baby won't feed from the breast, give her sips of this. It might help keep her strength up and will stop her dehydrating. It's what I gave my kids.' I handed over the bottles and added, 'It might be better not to tell Matron about this. It will most likely annoy her.'

We said goodnight and hurried off home. Later with the children in bed and the washing up done, I went out to look towards the little house in the back street. There were no lights or movement anywhere so I guessed that all was well and went to bed myself. I was almost asleep over my book when the car rattled up, its lights sweeping over the village, starting off the chorus of barking dogs that greeted any disturbance at night. I looked at the clock. It was almost eleven, an unearthly hour to be up at the Mission. By the time Neil and Laurie had shared out their catch and discussed the ones that got away I was too tired to give more than a fleeting thought to Cathie and her baby, except to feel a brief feeling of complacency. I had done all I could.

I was soon to regret my smugness. The next morning I was surprised to see Shirley hurrying across the common. She drew me away from the verandah where the children were playing and into the empty lounge room.

'Something dreadful happened last night,' she whispered, her voice shaking with emotion. 'You know that girl who was here yesterday, the one with the sick baby? Well, the baby died last night.'

'Oh no — what happened? Did it die at home? Oh, poor Cathie!' I babbled on, incoherent with shock. 'When did it die?'

'That doesn't matter. I don't know what time it was . . . and it didn't die at home. It died on the way to hospital.' Shirley began to cry hysterically.

'So Len took it in after all,' I began, but she interrupted angrily.

'Please listen to me. I didn't tell Len; I thought the baby was all right. This is the worst part. Cathie and her boy-friend walked into town and the baby died on the way.'

We sat in silence stunned by the thought of that terrible

journey through the dark bush. Then Shirley began to speak in a flat monotone.

'I didn't say anything about the baby when Len came in last night. He was so tired and I thought the baby would be all right. It wasn't Len's fault. He would have driven in but I didn't know how sick it was. I was going to see it this morning.'

She sat staring unhappily at me. 'So you mustn't tell anyone that Cathie brought the baby over here yesterday afternoon. You must not say that I told her she couldn't have a ride to town.'

'Who could I tell? The Welfare Board or the police? They wouldn't listen to me and they wouldn't care anyhow. But what about Cathie and her family? They'll tell someone.'

'No-one will take any notice of them. No-one would believe what they said.' She rose to leave but turned back at the door. 'You know it wasn't my fault. I didn't know that the baby was so sick.'

She was right. She was untrained and totally inadequate to do the job she had been given. She was as bewildered as any of her charges, but I didn't think that then and let her walk off without any reassurance or sympathy. I was overwhelmed by the tragedy of the baby's death and could see only the picture of those two young kids walking through the dark with their dying baby. I felt guilty for doing nothing to help and I felt angry that such a situation could arise. I resolved that one day I would tell everyone about the things that happened and the conditions in which these people lived and died. It was not Shirley's fallibility that was to blame, but the inhumanity of a system that not only tolerated these conditions but carefully hid them from the rest of the world.

- 14 -
A Parting Shot

In the autumn of 1963 I found a way to tell everyone about the iniquities of the Welfare Board and the squalor in which its charges lived. I met a group of people who were influential, who had the capacity to reach a wide audience and the ability to tell the tale properly. They were journalists who had gathered in Yarrawina for the Centenary Celebrations that started on 10 May. A few Sydney papers evidently thought the event newsworthy enough to be recorded in their pages, most likely as an amusing, nostalgic look at the simple ways of the outback rustics. Our local paper had no doubts about the importance of the occasion and we read constantly of the preparations that were in train. The Centenary Committee urged the shopkeepers to smarten up their premises with a coat of paint, all citizens were requested to brighten up their houses and gardens and there was earnest debate on what to do about the empty shops. A lady wrote in recommending that one of these be let to the Aborigines for the week, on the condition that they paint it and put up appropriate decorations. They could sell 'boomerangs, feather flowers and carved emu eggs' she suggested. It would fill one of the unused buildings that were an embarrassing reminder of how the town had regressed from its palmy days as an important river port.

Neil had taught the history behind the Centenary, the white history of course, and his school children were agog with excitement. They knew about the explorers, the bushrangers and the Cobb and Co. coaches and now it was all to be re-enacted for their entertainment. Our children were equally enthusiastic and so was I. Any break in the routine was welcome and we looked forward to the big opening on the Saturday.

There was to be a procession with the usual floats, clowns and bands led by a real stagecoach. A genuine antique steam train full of dignitaries was to arrive at the station and there were wonderful rumours about bushrangers swooping down on the town. The rest of the celebrations – the debutants' ball, the picnic races and the gymkhana – were a little more exclusive, but on Saturday everyone would be there, squatter and slaughterman, black and white, all rubbing shoulders and enjoying the sights for free.

So I was annoyed when Neil arrived home on Friday to tell me he'd have to take a couple of carloads of school children to town in the morning. The gubby truck was to make only one trip in and that meant many would be left behind and he felt obliged to take the left-over children in his car. I agreed that it was important that no one missed out but, seeing my plans for an early arrival in town foiled, I railed angrily that we again had to make up for the meanness of the Welfare Board. I was more upset when I saw Len's blue car pull out from the Big House early next morning with its four occupants waving happily. It was followed by Archie driving the truck crammed with excited, noisy people. Then Neil left, the car stuffed with school children. I could see another group larking around in the school yard waiting for his return but the rest of Mission was almost deserted. Some of the older residents stood about and two or three women drifted past with a group of little children. They were obviously the losers in the race for seats or else had opted for staying at home rather than facing the trip in the back of the crowded truck.

I began the complicated routine well-known to mothers of young children, the juggling of bathing and dressing to ensure that the first ones out of the tub remained clean and uncrumpled while the last ones were processed. We were almost finished. The responsible twins, almost dressed, were watching over Megan, who was clad in her singlet and panties, while Peter wiped himself and I hauled Christopher from the bath. My hair was damp and I was wearing a very wet dressing gown and little else when a call from outside was followed by Beth announcing that we had visitors. I hurried out, hoping that nothing had happened to the unsupervised school children, to see a group of elegant people emerging from a taxi. My first impulse was to hide but they were already advancing up the path.

A charming young woman introduced herself as a reporter for one of the popular women's magazines, then presented her photographer and two other journalists from Sydney dailies. They'd arrived the day before and were looking for a bit of local colour and some unusual slants on the town and district. They'd been to the ancient stone fish traps and the old wharves, but still had an hour to fill in before the start of the grand parade. Someone had suggested a trip to the Aboriginal reserve and here they were. They'd seen the notice about getting permission to enter and had stopped at the office, but the whole place seemed deserted. The taxi-driver had suggested calling on us. I started to explain that I was merely the teacher's wife, quite outside the Welfare Board hierarchy, but then I realised what a golden opportunity this was. Here were the people I needed. They could write about the conditions here and the whole State would know. No-one could plead ignorance after this.

'Of course you can have a look round,' I announced. 'There are still quite a few of the people here today. Why don't you talk to them? Most of them are what are called 'indigents' and they would welcome any chance to speak to someone new as they rarely leave the reserve.'

Rushing on I began to describe the ration system. Then I mentioned the dirt floors, the water taps in the street, the fat-tin lamps and the lack of all but the most basic amenities. I couldn't resist a quick run-down on the damage done to the school by the loss of the assistant and finished with an assertion that these living conditions and the restrictions on personal liberty would not be tolerated if they were inflicted on any white group. The journalists asked pertinent questions and showed considerable interest.

'Do you think we could take some photos of the people and

their houses?' one man asked. 'I'd like a couple of interior shots if possible?'

'You could ask but I doubt if they'll allow you inside. These people have a lot of pride. But there is nothing to stop you taking exterior shots.'

I gestured towards the scene before us, the mean shacks squatting in their bare yards with the morning sun highlighting their rusty iron and broken fibro. 'Now that would make a dramatic picture,' I added. 'Especially if you position it beside one of the Manager's residence.'

They looked towards the Big House standing like a green oasis in the dusty ochre of the reserve and agreed enthusiastically. As they moved off towards the waiting taxi they halted and turned.

'We've got a box of fruit in the car,' one said. 'Is it all right to give it to the people over there to be shared out?' When I assured him that it was indeed all right, he continued, 'Would you kiddies like some?'

I refused politely on their behalf, but as I looked at the naked boys and their half-clad sisters posed against the background of peeling paint and torn fly-wire and thought of my own unprepossessing appearance I wondered if our visitors might be considering an article on poverty-stricken teachers. The children were fascinated. They had rarely seen a white person in this setting and were overawed by these stylish creatures with their big cameras and their lavish offers of fruit. I jubilantly watched them walking round the miserable village. They carried their notebooks and cameras and were surrounded by an eager and co-operative crowd. I could almost envisage the articles they would write, the photos they would print and the unholy row that would follow the publication of this revelation of prejudice and neglect.

Then the taxi went away with a tail-end of children skipping behind, clutching peaches and pears with both hands. Neil drove in and hurriedly loaded up the remaining school children and we settled down to wait for his return. At last we set off, arriving in the main street as the tail end of the parade wound out of sight. The children hardly realised we'd missed it, entranced as they were by the clowns who darted about handing out balloons, the men on towering stilts and a hessian horse that gambolled and bucked right in front of us. We found the stagecoach with its magnificently bearded driver and guard and then hurried off to the railway station determined to be in time for this part of the entertainment. The steam train tooted triumphantly as it chuffed towards the station, but it was eclipsed by the glory of the gang of wild, hirsute bushrangers who galloped recklessly alongside, guns blazing. The children were hysterical with delight and fear. Megan scrambled up to hide her face in my neck and one of Neil's toughest little kindergarten boys gave an almighty wail and leapt up into the safety of Sir's arms.

The rest of the day passed in a whirl of noise and colour with bands and side-shows and bizarre costumes all vying for our attention. By three o'clock we were all exhausted. Neil set off to round up his passengers while the children and I sat in the park listening to the skirling of bagpipes competing with the twanging guitar of a cowboy who wandered around singing mournfully of his lost sweetheart. At four o'clock Neil re-appeared. He had driven home the four or five who were ready and waiting and Archie had promised to look after the rest. Many of his passengers had opted to stay in town overnight, so he had plenty of room. We thankfully drove back to the Mission. The children were drooping, worn out by a surfeit of excitement, ice-creams and fairy floss. We carried them inside, wiped off the surface dirt and put them to bed.

We were sitting with our feet up on the ledge of the stove enjoying its mild warmth and sipping a reviving drink when swift footsteps sounded on the path. The door was pushed open and Len strode in. Without any polite preambles, he asked how I dared to give permission for unauthorised persons to enter the reserve. I answered that as there was no-one else around I had taken it upon myself. After all, I could see no harm in allowing a few people to visit the place and hand out fruit to the children, I added lamely.

'You knew they were reporters,' he stated angrily. 'They should have been referred to Departmental officers.'

'There were none around,' I snapped back, my pugnacious

nature reasserting itself at his hectoring tone. 'If I'd sent them away they would naturally have assumed that there was something to hide. The Board isn't ashamed of the place, is it?'

He ranted about his job being made impossible because of our interference and we gathered that one of the higher Welfare Board officers had been interviewed by a reporter and the anger and bucket-tipping had passed down the line to Len. When Neil intervened mildly to suggest that any publicity was helpful and could only result in increased government spending, Len repeated his warning that our interference in Welfare matters would rebound on our heads and left.

We saw Len only once after that when he introduced the new manager and his wife. He had been transferred to a more favourable area to take up a new and interesting job. There were no effusive goodbyes and we were sorry that our association had ended so coldly. I am sure that they were glad to part both from us and from that area, where neither had been happy. His appointment as Manager of the Mission had no doubt been a step in the right direction, but at that time he was breaking new ground and was resented by many Aborigines, in town as well as on the reserve. He was seen as a sort of Uncle Tom who had sold out to the very body that was oppressing his brothers and sisters. Today the Aborigines expect to be represented only by their own people, but thirty years ago they were as biased as the whites against anyone who stepped outside the accepted stereotypes.

We waited excitedly for the publication of an article about the Mission. We searched the relevant Sydney papers and even ordered the next few copies of the women's magazine, much to the surprise of our newsagent who was quite amused when we told him the reason for our sudden obsessive interest. The town's festivities got a short mention in each paper. There were articles about the parade, the winner of the best beard competition and the Centenary Queen, who turned out to be the girl sponsored by the pastoralists, of course. We read about the ball, the bushrangers, the events at the gymkhana and even a short history of the district. The magazine gave the widest coverage, with two pages of glossy pictures and articles about the celebrations, the laid-back atmosphere of the district and its characters. Most of those mentioned did not live in the town itself, let alone on the river bank or the reserve. The only mention of anything Aboriginal was a sentence or two about the stone fish traps that had been constructed hundreds of years ago.

We were forced to accept that stories about Aborigines were not newsworthy. Hundreds of blacks living in squalid conditions rated nothing beside two white socialites who died in sordid circumstances. The Bogle-Chandler murder case was being tried in Sydney and its salacious details dominated the newspapers for weeks. So we gave up looking for revelations of man's inhumanity to man. Probably the heavy hand of the relevant government department had leant on the various editors to suppress the articles, but the most likely explanation was that, as no-one else had ever shown the slightest interest in stories we told about the Mission, why should these reporters and their editors be exceptions? They knew what would sell, and the ongoing, daily crimes against Aborigines had never made headlines in Australia.

The May holidays started shortly afterwards and they were particularly pleasant and peaceful. It was perfect autumn weather. The days were sunny and the river still warm enough for swimming while the cool nights invited the luxury of an occasional log fire. The mosquitoes were gone, the fish bit well and the vegetables flourished in our little garden. Neil spent hours preparing for the coming school term and together we made stencilled workbooks for his infant classes. The two weeks flew past and we looked forward optimistically to the rest of the winter. After the dramatic beginning to the year, life had settled down into an easy rhythm. The children were well, I felt better than I had for years and Neil was coping with the situation at school. My main worry was Kooka who was now too ill to visit, but everyone hoped that the cooler weather would improve her health. The people on the Mission seemed quietly content. The new Manager and his wife appeared fair and agreeable. We rarely saw them but the absence of angry outbursts and under-currents of ill-feeling augured well for a peaceful year.

Then Neil hurried home one afternoon at the end of May with

some startling news. He had received an offer of a school in the Riverina. It was the same grade as this one but it, of course, had an assistant. We had only a couple of days in which to decide and so he rang the Department and the principal of the new school for information. It was rumoured that the Mission school would be reclassified at the end of the year and the super-primary children in future would be driven into town each day. So Neil could no longer hold this position without dropping back a grade. We would have to leave in six months anyhow. The thought of the little town in the south was depressing, as it seemed the epitome of all we had vowed to avoid. It was a village in the wheat belt, a few houses clustered along a major interstate highway where the winters were cold and wet, and the summers dry and hot.

We argued and agonised for hours that night. I could not bear the thoughts of exchanging our unconventional and unusual surroundings for the prosaic staidness of an ordinary country town. We would get a vastly better house but it would overlook a bitumen road and a railway line instead of a wide brown river; we would be hemmed in by flat, cultivated farms instead of miles of unfenced bush. Worst of all, we would lose our diverse, idiosyncratic neighbours with their spontaneous warmth and their unpredictable behaviour for a bunch of stolid farmers. But then we were always brought back to the school situation. With no hope now of an assistant, Neil faced six months of drudgery. He would get nowhere in the field of Aboriginal education and this unexpected, unusual transfer in mid-year seemed to indicate that the Department of Education preferred that he be removed to a less controversial position. As Len had warned, it didn't do to be too open in expressing disapproval of a Government department.

I was preoccupied with the problem all next day and by the time a distant burst of shouting and laughter from across the common marked the end of the school day, I was still unable to accept the inevitable. Then the two girls came in from school. Beth wore her distant, haughty expression that denoted she was not pleased with the world.

'Daddy was very rude to me at school,' she announced. 'He roused on me and screwed up my stencil.'

'And he was cranky just because Beth coloured the duck blue instead of yellow. And she's the best colourer-in in Kindy and the best reader too,' Anne joined in loyally, her green eyes wide with indignation.

'Never mind, Beth,' I soothed 'Daddy has got a lot of worries at school now. Both of you get changed and go and play.'

They pulled on their shorts and tee-shirts, ate their afternoon tea and started off to join the others who were gambolling about in the dust near Green's house. At the gate Beth turned.

'I don't like yellow, you know,' she said gravely. 'I much prefer blue.'

When Neil walked in later, he too looked disgruntled. 'Did you have a bad day?' I asked.

'Bloody bad,' he announced 'Two fights, one pair of wet pants, a broken window and a bloody irate parent. I tell you what, Pat, I've had this job. It's impossible. There is no time to teach.'

'Well, you had better go and send that wire accepting the transfer. If we've got to go at Christmas time anyhow there is not much use in prolonging the agony. We might as well get it over with.'

'Right,' he said, glanced at his watch and strode towards the office. I sat at the table, poured a cup of tea and burst into tears. I decided to tell the children that evening as we were to leave the next week and at five o'clock I went into the yard to call them. The sun, slanting through the dust threw a golden haze over the village, softening the harsh outlines and disguising the ugliness of the houses. I could see Megan and Christopher darting around shrieking with laughter as they were chased by a bunyip in the guise of young Brian wearing a sugar bag on his head. Anne and Beth played skipping games with Patsy and Robin and Mrs Green watched from her step. She gave them a pat and a cuddle and shooed them home as I called. Allan relayed my message up the road.

'Peter, yer Mum wants you,' he shouted and in a few minutes Pete strolled down from the furthest group of houses. The village magpie sat on his forearm and his head bent towards it lovingly.

Their mutual devotion had begun not long after we arrived and though it flew home to old Mrs McHughes' house each night, it spent most of its days with Peter. I felt sick as I wondered how the children would react to the news that they must leave this place they loved so much, peopled with kind, amusing friends, where they roamed without fear of rebuff or risk.

We told them our news as they ate their evening meal and to our surprise they received it with that phlegmatic acceptance of adult decisions common to children young enough to still believe in their parent's wisdom. It was not until we had begun to pack away their toys and clothes in boxes a few days later that they really believed that this was not going to be just another holiday trip and that we would not be coming back. Anne and Beth worried about leaving their familiar little school group and Peter joined them in woeful litanies of people and places they would miss, but those three were old enough to be distracted by speculations about new friends and different activities. Megan was too young to do more than delight in the chaos of packing and happily impeded all my efforts to sort our belongings in an orderly manner. But Christopher sat in the midst of the turmoil like a figure of doom. He refused to discuss the move and clung to his possessions with a grim determination.

'This is *my* house,' he would reiterate stonily whenever we mentioned the journey and our future home. He would stare into space clutching his bubby blanket and I feared that he was remembering that ward full of strangers and the loss of all he had loved.

Neil cleared out his office at school and we fininshed sorting our belongings ready for the removalist. I was cleaning out the fridge when I realised that we would not need this kerosene model any more. We had wondered what we could give Mrs Green to show how much we appreciated all the care and affection she had showered on us, and I knew instantly what to do with the fridge. I ran over to her house to ask her if she would mind taking it. It would be something to remember us by, I added diffidently.

'I won't need anything to help remember you lot,' she smiled.

'And I hope you don't think I want something as a reward for doing my work, but yes, I'll be real happy to have a fridge again. I can keep the food from going bad, not just ours either. We'll all be able to use it.'

So we arranged that the boys would pick it up next day but that afternoon the clouds massed over the Mission and a deluge poured down. It was not possible to drive out of the yard let alone embark on a journey. Neil rang frantically, postponing the removalist and warning the Department that he couldn't take up the new appointment on schedule. So we began another wet weather stint, drying clothes by the fire, making dampers and worst of all unpacking food and clothes we'd put away so carefully in boxes. Tempers were very frayed by the time the sun returned to dry out the roads sufficiently for a trip to town to replenish our stocks. Neil re-booked the furniture truck two days hence.

We woke early Friday morning, ate a hasty breakfast and finished packing the car. We'd been around the village the evening before saying our painful farewells and there was nothing to do until the van arrived. The house already had a half-abandoned look, with the cupboards standing empty, the beds stripped and a regiment of boxes lined up in the hallway. I stood on the verandah looking down on the river. The brown water gleamed against the high bank opposite and a duck honked mournfully as it flew upstream and landed with scarcely a ripple. I thought of the first morning when that same view had cheered us and vanquished our fears about this strange new place. It seemed incredible that it was only eighteen months ago. We seemed to have crammed years of living into such a short time.

The van roared up and two cheerful men came in and assured us that they would be ready to meet us in our new house next morning. They were driving straight through, while we were going to stop overnight at Parkes, as the Department was paying for a motel room. With our record we should have known better than to believe fate would allow that simple plan to proceed. The storm that broke over Yarrawina later did not affect us, as we were well down the bitumen by that time, but it did hold up the furniture truck for two days while we languished in an empty house in a cold, strange town.

But now we were leaving. The children had gone out in the car and we hurried after them hoping to make a quick and unobtrusive departure. That was a vain wish. The yard seemed full of people: the school pupils, the women who had been our main support, a sprinkling of the older men and women and our little band of pre-school ragamuffins all stood grinning up at us. Mrs Green was nursing a bewildered Megan, while Mervyn and his teenage friends had taken charge of the other children. Someone evidently had planned a farewell surprise for us. My heart sank. This was a bit like that first night when we had stood before a similar, silent group. The same dark faces looked at us but they were no longer anonymous black people. They were now a group of friends we were going to leave forever and I feared that my cheerful facade would crack.

Then Peter Doolan stepped forward. 'We just want to say goodbye,' he said simply, 'and to wish you well in your new home.'

That broke the ice and everyone began to talk at once. We moved about, promising to write, to come back and visit and saying all those things that help us endure such partings. Then there was a rustle of anticipation and a murmur passed through the crowd. Heads turned towards the common and we followed their gaze. Grandma Boney, our beloved Kooka, was walking slowly across towards us. She was leaning heavily on Archie's arm and her beautiful grand-daughter, Princess Pat, walked alongside holding the wolfhound on its leash. We all waited in silence as she made her regal entrance. I knew she was sick and had given up hope of seeing her, contenting myself with sending a farewell letter and a present the day before.

It was overwhelming to see that small figure moving so slowly and painfully, and I knew that the people gathered in our yard were there to please her as well as to pay tribute to us. I have never felt so honoured as I did then and the long-threatened tears began to roll down my face. Those three, the mother, son and grand-daughter epitomised all the proud qualities of the Aborigines. We gathered the children and went to meet her.

'I've come to say good-bye too. I couldn't let my friends go without seeing old Kooka.' She chuckled softly and then bent towards the children. 'Good-bye, little fellers. You aren't scared of me and my big dog no more, are you? Good-bye Mr Keating. You did a real good job.' She clung to his hand a minute and then turned to me. 'Hey, where's all that laughing and talking got to? That's not my girl is it, crying like a baby? I kissed her wrinkled black cheek and she hugged me towards her for a moment.

'Go now, but don't forget us,' she said gently and turned away. We got into the car and as we drove out the gate a chorus of farewells and good wishes followed us. The children answered fervently, but Neil and I could only wave mutely. I saw Myrtle Green standing half-way between our two houses, one arm raised up in salute and when I saw that tears were running down her cheeks, I covered my face and wept silently. Her sturdy, indomitable figure was the last picture I had of the Mission. We had been given a glimpse of another way of life and we had met friends who remain as vividly in our minds now as they did on that cold June morning.

No, Kooka, we will never forget.

Pat, 1962